Thoughts on *Thought from the Bedside: From Medicine to Chaplaincy and Beyond*

Thank God for the entwined, challenging paths that brought Bill Holmes to scribble his thoughts and then do the tough work to organize, clarify, and edit them. Three unique perspectives mesh together over decades of personal and professional struggle to reflect upon the essence of life's fundamental concerns. Dr. Holmes gathers thoughts from medicine, ministry and personal crises on a wide range of crucial topics. His raw, vulnerable sharing allows us to peer beyond his thought into his heart throughout his painful personal search for balance, identity, mission, healing, and meaning. As he "leans in" to experience the patient as a whole person, he honors the worth of the "least of these" and elevates the marginalized to near sainthood.

He looks at life, death, cancer, community, racism, and poverty as a pediatric neurologist, a healthcare chaplain, and four time cancer survivor. Scripture, theology, and spiritual formation support his thoughts across the pages. With courage Bill introduces us to suffering patients as he reflects upon heaven, hope, faith struggles, miracles, and prayer. His compelling story is worth the investment, but his vision, assessments, commitments, wisdom and call for justice make it a must read for reflective health care providers, clinical clergy, struggling patients, and anxious families. This piece is not intended to be a textbook on any subject; nevertheless, students of many disciplines will find this writing informative, inspiring, and troubling. I know I did!

G. Wade Rowatt, Ph.D.
Senior Professor of Pastoral Care and Counseling
Baptist Seminary of Kentucky
ACPE Supervisor (Clinical Educator)

D1430397

Thoughts from the Bedside

FROM MEDICINE TO CHAPLAINCY AND BEYOND

Bill Holmes, M.D., M.Div.

Foreword by Walter Brueggemann

© 2018

Published in the United States by Nurturing Faith Inc., Macon GA,

www.nurturingfaith.net.

Library of Congress Cataloging-in-Publication Data is available.

ISBN 978-1-63528-032-6

Cover photo by LightFieldStudios.

This book is dedicated to the Rev. Dr. Dean K. Thompson, President Emeritus and Professor of Ministry Emeritus, Louisville Presbyterian Theological Seminary. He saw where I was heading before I did.

Contents

Foreword

Bill Holmes has strong professional credentials and a drawer full of degrees. It is clear in this manuscript, however, that what is interesting and compelling about Holmes is not his credentials or his degrees. What is compelling is the unmistakable fact that he is "all in." He is all in as a pediatric neurologist who has brought his expertise to children for whom he has cared. He is all in as a pastoral chaplain who sees persons whole, and who listens them to wellbeing. He is all in in his passion for justice and the urgency of compassion as he ponders the forces of racism and inequality that are so visible among us. He is all in with his illness, carrier of four different cancers. He is all in with his life that is a living testimony the way in which he has been a "man for others."

This statement by Holmes is an unguarded journal of his reflective life. It comes with deep personal honesty, with whimsical reflectiveness, and without sentimentality. Holmes understands so well that a transparent life is a life with transformative energy. Other readers will find, as I have found, that as Holmes lets us see his internal workings we become more self-aware and see ourselves more clearly. As he offers us a window to his self, so he is also a mirror for our selves.

The themes that Holmes takes up seem almost random, whatever is on his mind at the time. But when he gets to a theme he stays with it, drills down into it so that it yields some new awareness for him. Thus for example, he revisits his old home place on Brook Street and is aware that urban planning ravished his neighborhood. He sees beyond his own experience, that the fierce force of racism has been at work so that many others have suffered displacement and a savaging of the environment as well as safe living space. As elsewhere he moves beyond his own pathos about such loss to see the wider implications for those more vulnerable than he is.

Alongside his passion for justice and alertness to the viciousness of injustice is a bed-side availability that permits him to tell stories about specific persons with whom he has ministered. I am moved by the way he mobilized scripture to put together a prayer for the Emergency Department that moves in and out of the majestic Psalm 139. Holmes offers an extended riff on prayer, on the God to whom we pray, when to pray, and what to say. He shares memories of his growing up when he was nurtured in prayer, though he was drawn to a religious dimension of life by the prospect of being on the church basketball team. And for all of his intellectual sophistication he does not lose sight of the concrete reality of actual human persons in actual crisis situations who need and want to pray. He tells of praying with and being prayed for by a woman who faced imminent death by ovarian cancer. Given her own crisis, she nonetheless prayed for him as he faced a bone marrow procedure. Holmes has the grace to wonder how she was able to do that in the face of her own demise.

Holmes compromises none of his professional competence, either medical or pastoral. What comes through, however, is this authentic human being who has a sense of the ineffable in his own life, who is dazzled by the way that holiness shows up in quotidian ways, and that the ineffable is a crucial match for his own vulnerability. Holmes remembers in eloquent ways where he came from, knows some of his vulnerabilities, and in a more-or-less innocent way is able to trust the claims of faith and witness of scripture. When he comes to his own bouts with cancer, he has the good mature sense to reflect on the fact that he is "white, wealthy, and well insured" and so receives good care. Pushing promptly beyond himself, he wonders how it is for those who do not have such privilege and advantage as has he.

There are many matters to cherish in this honest book. One in particular has compelling force for me. When he received his diagnosis of multiple myeloma he replied with a poem as he sat on his deck watching rabbits and squirrels. The poem reports on the permission he gave to deer, wild rabbits, raccoons, a robin, some chipmunks, squirrels and bees to help themselves to the bounty of nature. The poem exudes generosity that permeates Bill's life and self-understanding.

It is worth reflecting, given this moving manuscript, how it is that in our society of busy, demanding technological reductionism, there can be an authentic human self who can be effectively present to others and flourish. I do not suggest that Bill is a model for anyone else. But he is a witness. He is a witness to the reality of humanity when it is refracted through the truth of the gospel. I anticipate that readers will relish this book in the way I have come to relish my times with Bill, a witty, generous human person among us who makes a difference under the cover of his several degrees.

Walter Brueggemann
Columbia Theological Seminary

Acknowledgments

My first attempts at expressing my spiritual concerns and thoughts on paper were in the form of sermons written as pastor of Mount Lebanon Presbyterian Church (MLP) in north Clark County, Indiana. I am forever indebted to the membership of MLP for their faith and trust in me; they were my teachers for two years and beyond.

I am grateful to Dr. J. Brad Wigger, the Louisville Seminary, and the Collegeville Institute for inviting me to participate in the Writing Workshop for Pastors.

For reading and critiquing my manuscript, I am grateful to Dr. Wade Rowatt, professor of pastoral care at the Baptist Seminary of Kentucky; and Rev. Kerry Wentworth, my fellow chaplain and mentor at Norton Brownsboro Hospital in Louisville.

I am indebted to Rev. Dr. Ronald Oliver, system vice president for mission and outreach at Norton Healthcare, for inviting me to share in the ministry of chaplaincy. I am forever grateful to Rev. Kelley Woggon, who by her example taught me to remove obstructions to listening and then lean in so as to hear the voices of the suffering.

My life has been deeply affected by the ministry of Rev. Dr. Joe Phelps, pastor of Highland Baptist Church (HBC) of Louisville. He not only led the church to ordain me to the ministry of Jesus Christ but also challenged me to speak out against injustice. He also introduced me to Walter Brueggemann, who by his words, his many books and articles, and his actions has been a constant inspiration in all that I have done over the last decade.

Some of my essays, reflections, and ideas in this book are reproduced in whole or in part, with permission, from articles that were first published in the following publications:

- *Church Health Reader*, a publication of the Church Health Center, Memphis, Tennessee. Both the *Reader* and the center, founded by Dr. G. Scott Morris, have a unique ministry that reaches well beyond Memphis.

- *Word and World*, a publication of Luther Seminary, St. Paul, Minnesota. Thanks also to Dr. Fred Gaiser, the immediate past editor, who invited me to contribute.
- *EthicsDaily.com*, a division of the Baptist Center for Ethics, Nashville, Tennessee. I am grateful to Zach Dawes and to the late Robert Parham, who founded and directed the center.
- *The Oates Journal* (online), a publication of the Wayne E. Oates Foundation, Louisville, Kentucky. Please read my tribute in this book to the late Christopher A. Hammond, past director of the foundation.

I am more than grateful to my wife of forty-nine years, Joyce Lynn Yates Holmes, for giving me space and encouraging me during long hours in my study. My gratitude extends to my daughters, Suzanne Bowman and Emily Brown, who even as children gave me space to read and write. When I was doing postgraduate work in neurology, Emily's teacher asked her what her daddy did for a living. Emily replied, "He reads books." Well, now he has written one.

Preface

Most of this book was not written with a book in mind. I made notes during the quiet of the evening or early morning hours while reflecting on the encounters of the day. Over the years I have kept my notes in a loose-leaf binder labeled "Scribblings," my thoughts from the bedside of those struggling to find meaning in the midst of suffering.

I intend "bedside" to be a metaphor for that place where we are called to engage all that we are on behalf of the one who is in a place of disorientation, where things are not as they were and likely never will be again. In some cases things have never been as they should be, for injustice has made its mark on the one who sits in front of me. In all such places hope struggles to be redefined. It is at such times that questions arise concerning death, dying, afterlife, miracles, and prayer.

What ultimately generated my desire to write this book was an emerging awareness of the intertwining of my life with all who take this journey. Sharing in the suffering of others has given my life a deeper meaning than it might have otherwise attained. The nature of the suffering might be a physical or medical condition such as cancer or disabilities, coping with loss, depression, social injustice (including racism), as well as living in isolation or in a void created out of collusion between humankind and technology.

I have drawn on a variety of experiences from seven years in general pediatrics and thirty years in child and adult neurology followed by six years in hospital chaplaincy. I am amazed by the way my fellow travelers keep going in the face of the unspeakable, including cancer, chronic neurological diseases, and a litany of conditions and diseases.

Over the years I have been deeply moved by the exemplary lives of parents, nurses, and my fellow chaplains and physicians. In addition, the inspiration to write arose out of my encounters with social injustice and suffering that first barged into my awareness in my preadolescent and adolescent years.

Sometimes it is just the unwanted stuff of everyday life that comes without invitation to threaten us on the one hand but with the potential to make us better servants and caregivers on the other.

Along the way I have stacked stones here and there to mark my encounters with stories that changed who I am and how I perceive life itself. One such marker came as a teenager when the powers-that-be destroyed the quiet beauty of our street and then built an interstate highway in front of our home and an off-ramp through our backyard within thirty feet of my bedroom window. Another stack of stones came years later when a young epileptic child fell to one side while sitting in front of me and unwittingly marked the beginning of my journey toward the practice and teaching of neurology. Still a decade later a gay man with headaches would come seeking my help. His journey into isolation and death secondary to HIV/AIDS reverberates still in my deepest memories.

I have also written with the cancer sufferer in mind not only because of my personal encounters with cancer but also due to an overwhelming image that hovers in and around me and will not let me go. A few days before his death I visited William T. (Bill) Applegate, my high school classmate and friend. Bill voiced no complaint even though he was most certainly in incredible pain. He reached out to me with his right hand and asked how I was doing. Bill Applegate was in dying as he was in living.

Soon after I started my work as a hospital chaplain, I stood at the bedside with the family of a brain-dead man as he was removed from life support. It was a moment of epiphany as I began to see life and death from the other side of the reflex hammer where most of my fellow travelers stand. What happens at the bedside is often more than we initially see. What is needed is a different lens, a different way of looking at human suffering, so that which we have beheld as a clinical observer becomes a divine encounter.

With each essay, reflection, and poetic writing I intend to speak of the need for our presence in community with the suffering. Even then there is more than a human presence, for in all such instances God is also present. This presence acting in the world is not dependent in any way on whether or not we see or acknowledge it. God spoke first; God will have the last word: "In the beginning was the Word" (John 1:1).

I am accustomed to being awake at all hours of the night. I am well practiced due to my work in medicine and chaplaincy. Somewhere past midnight I often reflect on my life as it has been, on the experiences that will never let me go and now have become the subject matter of my writing.

There is a lot going on at 4 a.m., most of it in my head. Nonetheless, there is a reality that speaks to the moment.

Four Past Midnight

Infants cry out
Mothers do what mothers do

The Spirit speaks
The soul hears silence

Prophets lament and wail
Deaf ears turn and sleep

Agonal breaths quicken
Vigils are kept

Reason takes its leave
Would-be poets scribble

Bill Holmes
4:24 a.m.
September 3, 2014

NORTON
BROWNSBORO HOSPITAL

1707

Pastoral Care

Rev. Kerry M. Wentworth,
M.Div., MBA, BCC
Rev. Bill Holmes,
MD, M.Div.

Chaplains' Office (Norton Brownsboro Hospital)

CHAPTER 1

A Retired Child Neurologist
Becomes a Chaplain

My calendar entries for the week: Wednesday, 11 a.m., memorial service; Friday, 5:30 p.m., rehearsal; Saturday, 4 p.m., wedding. The memorial service was for a man who had died in the hospital where I serve as chaplain. I had come to know him over the span of several months and multiple hospital admissions. Over the course of his prolonged final hospital stay, his family began to refer to me as their "hospital pastor," a title I was honored to bear. He had no other pastor, as he was not strongly attached to any church and had put "none" in the religious preference box at admission. However, like so many others who self-identify as "no religious preference" or "none," he was a man who had been on a faith journey, albeit a stormy one.

I was with him and his family when he took his final breath. I later visited with them at the funeral home, something I do from time to time. I was warmly greeted and embraced. His widow then said, "We need some words said over him and some Bible verses read." When needed, those are the things I now do, and so I did. I helped with the memorial service at the funeral home and did the graveside remarks and closing prayer. It was a chilly and very rainy afternoon. I stood in about an inch of water as I read from John's Gospel and prayed. My shoes were muddy, and my trouser cuffs were wet as I headed for my pickup truck—and I was feeling thankful and blessed.

The wedding was that of a young lady who had been my patient several years ago. She had called months before the wedding to ask if I would mind doing the ceremony. Mind? I was delighted and felt it an honor to be asked. The bride-to-be's sister had also been my patient for many years. She was severely impaired and had never walked or talked. Her seizures were frequent and never totally controlled. I think she is alive largely due to the incredible loving care given by her parents and, as I recall, her grandparents. I have many stories of dedicated parents and grandparents heroically giving their all to give a severely impaired child the best life possible considering the circumstances. Hers was such a family.

The bride and groom wanted to be married in a backyard ceremony at her grandparents' home. We met a few weeks before the wedding to discuss their commitment to each other as well as the specifics of the wedding. It was a warm summer evening when their families and friends gathered to witness their vows. I was told by one of the guests who is also a longtime friend that I looked calm and relaxed. Little did he or anyone else know that this was only my third time to preside at a wedding and I was anything but calm on the inside. Nonetheless, no one seemed to notice my uncertainty.

Seventy-plus years ago my parents probably never thought I would be doing such things one day. They just hoped my behavior would not land me in jail. My mastering of four-letter words led to my being banned from more yards and playgrounds than imaginable, and that by the age of six years. So bad was the outpouring of profanity from my lips that even the street's edge in front of some of my friends' homes became off-limits. Watching my peers play baseball from the middle of the street became a habit. Viewing life from the white line on an asphalt road can present challenges. Being an "outsider" of a sort is always difficult but is particularly problematic in the preteen years. Such was my place in the community until my family moved into the city to a rented apartment on South Brook Street when I was eleven years old.

We had moved to a neighborhood in transition from a predominantly white middle-class one with a large Jewish population to one that had an increasing number of renters and apartment dwellers who were somewhat migratory, as were we. With that transition came more family instability, gangs, and a good deal of uncertainty both for the community and for me personally. In my early teens refocusing and redirecting became a dynamic and never-ending process carried out under sometimes difficult conditions, much like having eighteen-wheelers passing me on both sides of the road simultaneously. I learned early to observe closely and react quickly.

Even as I looked down the road in great anticipation of what might be next, I knew that I was likely to wander off, look around for I-know-not-what, then, thankful that I was not run over, feel my way back to a bumpy, pothole-marked road that never looked totally familiar. At times I chose to follow a road that went nowhere or threatened to be more than I could handle. My wanderings off the path became my unexpected teachers. At each step along the way, from deep within me, and sometimes from without, I heard, "You can't do that!" and "No, you are not." But counterarguments came as well, saying, "Yes, you can; yes, you are."

The road I have taken since leaving Brook Street was not planned with a Google Map or AAA. "You are here" marked the starting point, but where was "here"? I did not set out with a plan to start my theological and pastoral care education, drop out to go to medical school, spend the next thirty-seven years in continuous learning, teaching, and practicing medicine, then return to seminary to complete my theological education and end up a hospital chaplain. Some have told me it was the hand of God leading me along this path. While that is a well-worn explanation for wilderness wanderings by indecisive people, I am not yet ready to hold God responsible for the path I took to this point.

My journey has been non-linear and driven at times by reasons of the heart rather than logic. Although I know little about hunting, I suspect I have been like an old coon dog who sniffs his way along the path but keeps wandering into the thicket for he-knows-not-what. Eventually I get to where I think I want to go, but the path is never straight.

During my college years the dynamics of faith in the lives of women and men, both the famous and the little known, became the focus of my inquiries as I sought to reinterpret the religion of my youth and redefine the role of faith in my life as a would-be healer. I read from a diverse group of writers. Carlyle Marney, Martin Buber, Hudson Taylor, and Elton Trueblood were the mainstays of my reading. Marney was a Baptist who thought and wrote ahead of his time; Buber was a Jewish philosopher whose 1923 book *I and Thou* captured the imagination of many even in the 1960s; Taylor was a British man who founded the China Inland Mission; and Trueblood was a Quaker scholar and theologian who taught at Earlham College, just north of where I grew up. Each contributed something to how I saw the world as I started the third decade of life.

Life can be such that your beginning becomes your end as well. It may well be that I have returned to where I was supposed to be all along. In a sense where I find myself today completes a circle originating in 1965 when I graduated from Vanderbilt University and started my theological education at Southern Baptist Theological Seminary in Louisville. Throughout my student years at Vanderbilt University, I maintained an interest in medicine and theology.

I majored in philosophy with a near major in chemistry; I was better at the latter. When I started seminary in fall 1965, my primary interest was in pastoral care and counseling, but I also considered teaching philosophy of religion. I had the privilege of studying with Dr. Wayne Oates, one of the early fathers of pastoral care and counseling. We looked closely at the works of Gordon Allport and Anton Boisen. My introduction to Boisen's works prompted me to recoil at first. His struggle with mental illness yielded unique insights that came to bear on his work as a hospital chaplain in the early twentieth century.[1]

Despite my intense interest in my seminary studies, the challenges of understanding and applying the sciences to human healing kept calling as a siren from the rocks. Whether intended or not, Dr. Oates played a significant part in what I saw as my calling to medicine, a calling I have since questioned again and again. Dr. Oates often stayed after class to be queried by his students. We had several conversations in late fall 1965. It was as though he knew before I knew that I was heading into medicine. It was after a prolonged conversation with Dr. Oates and later with Dr. G. David McClure that I decided to go on to medical school.

Dr. McClure had been my Sunday school teacher as a teen. He knew how to keep teens engaged. His Bible lessons were about five to ten minutes long. Then he threw it out to us with, "So what is happening?" or "What has this got to do with you?" No telling where those lessons would go, but we, a bunch of teenagers, stayed right there and voiced our opinions. The man you met in Sunday school was the man you met in his ophthalmology practice: brief and to the point. Not surprisingly he was also trained in law. I would accompany him to a class he taught on medical malpractice at the Brandeis School of Law since I knew how to operate a projector.

Even when I was sitting in his office having my eyes refracted, Dr. McClure would be teaching. Socrates would have been envious (no, I am not Plato). As he would click the last lens into place, he would ask, "How does the world look now?" Yes, the words had a double meaning. It was an invitation to say whatever. I always felt sorry for the one sitting patiently in the waiting room. I suspect that person learned the full meaning of *waiting*.

He also repeatedly reminded me that I had gifts, talents, and abilities I needed to find and use. He never let me forget such things. And when things did not go as planned, he said, "Sometimes our best is none too good." I heard that more than a few times as we sat in his study and discussed "Where to from here?" It was in that study in December 1965 that I became convinced it was time to leave seminary for medical school.

I regarded Dr. Oates' encouragement to pursue medicine and psychiatry as a sign of his confidence in my ability to succeed in this endeavor. Two of my closest friends are now pastoral care and counseling teachers who trained with Dr. Oates. They have jokingly (or maybe not) informed me that Dr. Oates was telling me I would not likely do well in his area of expertise. Perhaps they were more right than wrong.

I entered medical school with the intention of training in psychiatry. During medical school I worked two summers as a research assistant in psychiatry looking at the effect of multiple-monitored-electroconvulsive therapy (MMECT) on major depression. While so-called "shock therapy" does not sound appealing to most, in a day when there were fewer effective psychoactive drugs, MMECT proved to be useful in otherwise nearly hopeless cases. I also looked closely at the role of gamma-amino-butyric acid (GABA) in the central nervous system, a project that was capped off by listening to presentations of the most recent research on GABA at the New York Academy of Science meeting in New York City. I came away from that meeting convinced I would not do bench or basic research.

After an internship in general pediatrics at the University of Louisville School of Medicine and Kosair Children's Hospital, I started a psychiatry residency at Barnes and Renard Hospitals at Washington University School of Medicine, St. Louis. I had the best of teachers. The chief of psychiatry was Dr. Eli Robins, a brilliant man who stressed the need to do research and apply scientific thinking to the treatment of psychiatric disorders rather than follow Freudian thinking. I will never forget the first time I went into the restrooms in the doctor's lounge. There above two side-by-side urinals were the likenesses of Freud and Jung. The message was clear.

I lasted three months in psychiatry training. I had encountered a large psychotic man my first night on call. The next morning I sat for nearly two hours with a lady with an anxiety neurosis. Neither scenario appealed to me. For some reason I did not find it satisfying. So went most of my first months in training. After long discussion with my fellow residents, I decided to return to Louisville for further pediatric training. I had long been aware that being around kids was something I did with ease. As a teen I had volunteered in the church nursery changing diapers and rocking babies. As a junior counselor in summer camps during high school, I was called "Mother Bill" by some of the campers and my co-workers. No reason for this moniker was ever given. It should have been "Grandmother Bill" as, in a sense, pediatricians often function as grandmother-replacements in our society as they give advice on child rearing and offer a gentle touch to soothe wounded knees and egos.

But pediatrics is about more than just liking kids; it is about being fully invested in the health and welfare of the child. During my internship at Kosair Children's Hospital and beyond, I received inspiration from great teachers who brought alive the challenge of making an accurate and timely diagnosis. They were relentless in their pursuit of doing what was best for children and families. In addition, my professors were blind to social and financial status; the rich man's kids and the poor man's kids received the same focused attention and treatment.

A child I encountered as an intern played a significant role in setting the course of my professional life. Her mother brought her to the pediatric clinic wrapped in a blanket to protect her from the January winds blowing off the Ohio River. Although well past the age when walking is expected, she had to be carried. As her mother sat her on the exam table, her body began to tilt to the left, her head turned in the same direction, and all expression drained from her now flushed face. Saliva began to pour from the corner of her mouth. The episode ended within a minute only to be repeated several times over the next half hour. Little did I know at the time that a seed had been planted in my very being, which over the next few years would germinate, sprout, take root, and flourish.

The challenge of finding the reason for her epilepsy and an effective treatment was much greater in 1970–1971. There were no CT scans, no MRIs, and no myriad of readily available blood tests. A detailed medical history and a physical examination had not yet surrendered their position as the primary diagnostic tools in medicine. Treatment options were quite limited. Phenobarbital and Dilantin, both fraught with side effects, were the main anti-epileptic drugs of the day. Eventually she was put on both drugs before I lost track of her over the next year as her care was assumed by the neurology clinic.

I did not see the young lady with epilepsy again for about twenty years. By chance I was the on-call neurologist when she, suffering multiple seizures, was brought into the adult ER in the early morning hours. Her mother recognized me immediately, but the kid who unwittingly inspired me just smiled and started turning her head to the left. She never knew, nor would she have understood, the impact her suffering had had on me.

After two more years of postgraduate pediatric training, I practiced general pediatrics for four years. I saw an increasing number of kids with neurologic diseases. As a primary care physician for kids, I became more aware of the lack of fully trained pediatric neurologists locally and throughout the state. Subsequently, I decided to apply to several postgraduate training programs. I made plans to leave general pediatrics and go to Atlanta to train in child neurology, a move that would have been difficult on my family. In early January 1977 I received a call from Dr. David Barrett Clark, chairman of neurology at the University of Kentucky (UK), which was only eighty-five miles away. Dr. Clark, one of the founders of pediatric neurology in America, explained that he had an "unexpected opening." At the moment I did not know the significance of the phrase, but eventually I learned it was code for someone who could not take the rigors of the program and decided to leave. I drove to Lexington a few days later on a most memorable day as it was a record-cold ten degrees below zero, a temperature that my old Pontiac coupe found not to its liking. I had visions of being stranded on the frozen tundra of the Bluegrass Country.

When I headed to UK in June 1977 to begin my postgraduate training in neurology and child neurology, the memory of my first patient with epilepsy went with me. Dr. Clark knew I had dropped out of seminary to go to medical school. Throughout my training he referred to me as "Reverend Holmes," often deferring to me on religious and spiritual questions as if I knew what I was talking about. He would recommend that I do some "spiritual care" even as I was searching for a medical diagnosis and a suitable treatment. It is possible to do some pastoral care as a physician but not as much as some might think. As a physician I can offer care and concern, but it is quite a different thing to listen for no other reason than to allow the one suffering to say what is on his mind, and even more difficult to do so without thinking, "What is the diagnosis? How shall I treat this?"

My three years at the Albert Chandler Medical Center at UK not only shaped me as a neurologist but also had a significant effect on how I see the person on the other end of the reflex hammer. UK serves the central and eastern part of the state, better known as Appalachia. One of my greatest learning experiences was also a service opportunity. Monthly, we traveled to such places as Hazard, Paintsville, Pikeville, and Ashland. We arrived in the early morning and saw kids with neurological problems all day. Then we had dinner at a local establishment before bedding down for the night at the cheapest livable motel. The next morning we saw children until noon before turning homeward. What I learned in the clinic went beyond the presentation, natural history, and treatment of neurologic conditions; I also learned to hear the voice of poverty in Appalachia. What I heard and saw were not complaints about what they did not have, but a readiness to give out of their scarcity. The kids most often were not acutely aware of their lack of things and stuff. As one growing up in inner-city Louisville in near-poverty, I readily identified with them.

One thing that became apparent early on was the importance of faith for the mountain folks. The church with its hymns and prayers spoke to them of hope in the midst of difficult times full of hopelessness. Almost all came from conservative, if not fundamentalist, traditions. Pentecostalism was common among the families who brought their children to see us. Reliance on prayer was part and parcel of who they were. When the word spread that I had done some seminary work and a little preaching in rural Carter County when I was younger, the questions and requests for prayer came. On more than a few occasions the parents would lay hands on my arm or shoulder and start to pray out loud. Others in the room, usually a grandmother or older sibling, would then join in with "Amen!" and "Yes, Lord!"

For most of the Appalachian families I met, the elderly were held in high regard. In the 1970s nursing home placement was less common, probably for financial reasons as well as lack of availability. I did not take a poll, but my sense was that doing something other than keeping the aging person in the home was simply not the thing to do. On the day after Christmas 1977, I was called to the ER of the VA hospital to see a seventy-five-year-old man who had been "found down" in the barn on Christmas Eve. He was poorly responsive and had bruising on the left side of his head. In the late 1970s it took a few hours to complete a CT scan of the head. Since we suspected a subdural hematoma, we immediately performed a cerebral angiogram, which revealed displacement of the left cerebral vessels, a finding consistent with a subdural fluid collection. I scrubbed in with the neurosurgeon, who then, using his Black and Decker drill and a surgical saw blade to remove a section of the skull, removed the clot, placed a drain, and gave IV mannitol to reduce the brain swelling. It was not enough; he died forty-eight hours later from overwhelming infection in his lungs, a process that had no doubt started as he rested on the sofa at home for thirty-six hours.

I sat with the family for a long period that afternoon. They sensed that I was wondering why they took so long to get him to Lexington. I will never forget their unsolicited answer. As strange as it might seem to many, it was clearly their love and respect for him that prompted the delay in seeking care. They went on to tell me that a few years earlier their oldest brother had died at the VA hospital from a massive stroke. He had been kept alive on a ventilator for three days. Subsequently, their father had asked that such never be allowed to happen to him. As a family they felt they were honoring that request. I don't recall if I had any verbal response at all. I hope I did not, for there are times when silence is in order, and that was such a time.

In June 1980 I returned to Louisville and joined two adult neurologists in practice. Dr. Roy Meckler, a brilliant diagnostician, had been seeing a significant number of children and teenagers, as there were no child neurologists in full-time practice. Over the course of the next thirteen years, I did virtually all the child neurology at Children's Hospital except for one year when an excellent child neurologist joined the University of Louisville department of neurology. She agreed to cover the hospital workload with me on a part-time basis.

Kosair Children's (now Norton Children's), the hospital in which I practiced for most of my career, is a university-affiliated referral center and the regional pediatric trauma center. Children come from western and central Kentucky as well as southern Indiana. They are usually quite ill. Life-threatening illnesses and accidents are daily occurrences; the uncommon is common. The children of the working poor, uninsured children, and Medicaid-eligible kids made up well over half of our patient population. In the last two decades of the century, approximately twenty-five percent of children in Kentucky were living at or below the federally established poverty level. Failure to immunize and the lack of basic healthcare access contributed to the morbidity and mortality rate among kids.

On any given day the hospital waiting rooms and the foldout couches were full of anxious and grieving parents. As a physician I was sensitive to what was going on but had little time to deal in depth with the emotional, spiritual, and social side. Someone else had to take on those tasks. Children's Hospital and its parent, Norton Healthcare, have long been leaders in developing and maintaining the role of the chaplain in a hospital setting. One of the central concerns of Norton Healthcare is the spiritual needs of both the patients and the staff in the context of some of the greatest stresses they will ever face. It is for that very purpose that God created chaplains, or so it seems.

Not long ago at a national chaplains' meeting I encountered some angst on the part of several chaplains that they were respected neither by the administration nor the medical staff, raising concerns that they might be eliminated in the next budget cut. No one in the room knew at first that I was a retired physician who had become a chaplain. When my turn came to speak, I pointed to the list of chaplain duties listed in the PowerPoint. Number two was "Be a presence." Then I told of my experiences with the chaplains at Norton Hospital and Kosair Children's Hospital over a period of thirty-plus years. When I made ICU rounds early each morning, a chaplain was right there with us. When my patient was dying in the ICU at 2 a.m., I arrived to find a chaplain already ministering to the grieving family as well as the nurses who were also experiencing loss.

When major pediatric trauma victims arrived in the ER, there also was the chaplain. When my patient of many years succumbed to a degenerative neurologic disease, his family brought him to the ER before he drew his last breath. When I arrived at 4:30 a.m., the chaplain was already comforting the family; it was Christmas morning 1990. Also, early on Christmas Day 1992, a child with congenital heart disease suffered a major stoke. I was at the hospital by 7 a.m. and left at suppertime. Almost hourly the care team and I went to update the parents. And at every update there also was the ICU chaplain ministering to the family from dawn to dusk.

Finally, when I had surgery for removal of what prove to be the beginning of colon cancer and I was at one of the lowest ebbs of my life, there came to my bedside a chaplain. I recall nothing of what he said, but I remember well his comforting presence.

Don't believe for one minute that I as a physician did not respect our hospital chaplains. I did, and I do, so much so that I have become one. But becoming a chaplain is just the beginning of a journey that has either redefined or refined how I see what happens in bedside encounters, both past and present.

One of the most difficult tasks I have faced is moving away from thinking like a physician at the bedside. No longer is a detailed medical history needed.

No longer must my mind run through a list of possible diagnoses. No longer do I need to take out my Queen Square reflex hammer and assess the nervous system of the one lying in the bed. Now, I simply clear the clutter, lean in, and listen.

Note

[1]Anton Boisen, *Out of the Depths* (New York: Harper and Brothers, 1960).

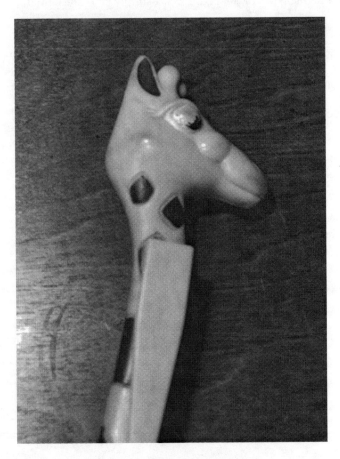

Giraffe Reflex Hammer
(Reflex hammer used in examining kids)

CHAPTER 2

Death and Dying

I have a habit of jotting down my thoughts on the blank pages of books or just inside the front cover. Sometimes I will record the date and time as well. In January 2002, about six months after heart surgery, I wrote the following words on a blank page in Martin Marty's *A Cry of Absence: Reflections for the Winter of the Heart*: "I no longer fear death. I have already done the difficult—I have lived. As for dying, that's another matter." I have found that talking about dying and death diminishes my anxiety, and writing about them helps even more. Nonetheless, I have had great difficulty putting my thoughts into words.

Dying starts at birth. A great deal of neuroscience research has been gathered in the last several decades on *apoptosis*, which is programmed cell death so that some nervous system cells start to die at birth. But beyond the scientific there is a sense in which much of life is spent wrestling with this reality. That the power of death is at work in the world is evident in many aspects of our lives. We use work and possessions to justify our existence. Even "non-work" experiences, especially when we perceive them as devoid of meaning, can be like waiting on death. For some the harshness of work may be so great that it is seen as a foretaste of death or nonexistence.

For the first thirteen years of medical practice, work justified my existence and defined who I was. I was known for being the first doctor in the hospital in the morning and the last to leave at night. On my scheduled afternoon off I felt empty, so much so that I often scheduled patients that I perceived as needing to be seen sooner. It was as though work was warding off any concerns about death, about nonexistence. To some extent the clinical stories that follow have served to put death at arm's length.

Just Like That and It's Over

Several years ago I stood at the bedside of an elderly woman who was in the last minutes of her life. Her son and her husband of sixty years stood opposite me.

She had somewhat labored breathing, the type one has just before the last breath is drawn. Soon she took a few agonal breaths, then ceased all signs of life. Her husband gasped and looked at me as if to ask, "What is happening?" I will never forget his arms flailing upward as he said, "You mean it is just like that and it is over? Just like that? Can't we have a few more minutes?"

How often from the waiting rooms and hallways of hospitals do I hear, "Let us hope she can rally again!" or "Is it really over?" The language of loss and the language of hope may, at times, come into conflict as we face end-of-life issues. Withdrawing treatment or life-support is often viewed as a defeat after "battling" an illness. Instead of recognition of a life well lived, the language of losing and winning takes center stage.

In our culture we are prone to do everything we can to continue life, sometimes even when life is clearly over. We place great hope and trust in modern medicine to sustain life. A heart can be kept beating for a long time after the brain has ceased to show any signs of functioning. We can and do keep on resuscitating even when it is clear that what is left is hardly recognizable as the person we knew and loved.

Acknowledging that death is unavoidably near changes the dynamics at the bedside. Often a family objects to talking about imminent death with a dying loved one. Many find it difficult to sit next to a dying friend knowing that that friend is cognizant of his imminent death. A certain discomfort may take hold, so we tend to leave the bedside of the dying as our discomfort with death overtakes us.

The dynamics of hope and a "hopeless" situation deserve our thought and prayer. Is it giving up hope to accept that the end of life has come? What is the basis of our hope as people of faith? On the one hand it is to the credit of modern medicine that death is held back for a spell. But unless there is some other non-medical response to the threat of death, some belief system that says death does not represent the finality of all there is, then death *does* win the day.

So when the brain waves cease and the heart takes its last beat, is there some foundation for hope? In church we tend to have easy, pat, and glib answers to such questions, but for many they tend not to fly well at the time of death, for it is there that grief must first do its work. Some well-meaning person may say, "He is with Jesus now" or "We will see him again in the resurrection." For many such is neither helpful to hear nor necessarily good theology.

Since our dying is a part of our lives, we must consider how we will leave this life. Hopefully the dying person will draw his last breath surrounded by loved ones, but such is not a given. We often die in specialized units that are dedicated to sustaining life. The well-trained medical staff is quite good at what they do, working diligently and with compassion. But "medicalized" dying, even that offered by hospice and palliative care, comes with a risk of loss of community for the dying person.

Somehow we in the church need to articulate clearly a theology of dying just as we have a theology for living. Hopefully pastors can help congregants deal with these difficult questions. However, our theology is often embedded from childhood and is simply not up to the task. Quoting a few scriptures will not get it done. From my observations at the bedside, there is serious reconsideration needed to what Scripture says or does not say about life after death, the meaning of salvation, resurrection, healing, and miracles. It is my hope that we might learn to live hopefully in the face of impending death, even our own. This is not an easy task!

Brain Death:
The View from the Other Side of the Reflex Hammer

There are events that come unexpectedly, defining and redefining our purposes, our goals, and our views of life and death. Encountering brain death for the first time as chaplain was such for me. I had not foreseen the impact the change from neurologist to chaplain would have on how I understand what is going on at the bedside. Things not visible to the human eye but more readily seen by the heart of humankind take center stage.

My Queen Square reflex hammer was my constant companion throughout thirty years of neurology practice. I used it daily to check reflexes as I sought to determine the neurologic status of those who entrusted me with their care. The hammer, which takes its name from Queen Square Hospital in London, was also used as one tool to assess for signs of life when brain death determination is performed. With children I used a different reflex hammer that looked like the neck and head of a giraffe.

In 1986 the Kentucky State Legislature passed a statute to define brain death legally.

Determination of death—Minimal conditions to be met

1. When respiration and circulation are not artificially maintained, there is an irreversible cessation of spontaneous respiration and circulation; or

2. When respiration and circulation are artificially maintained, and there is a total and irreversible cessation of all brain function, including the brain stem and that such determination is made by two (2) licensed physicians.[1]

The law requires no particular tests. Usually a detailed neurological exam reveals the following: dilated pupils, unreactive to even the strongest light; no movement of the eyes when the head is passively turned; no blink when the cornea is touched by a cotton wisp; and no reflexes when the knees or other joints are tapped with a reflex hammer. At the time of determination of brain death, body temperature must be normal, and no medication in high enough level to cause sedation can be in the blood. In all cases, by law, the Kentucky Organ Donor Association is contacted to see if organ donation is possible.

As a neurologist I was often called to the ICU to confirm brain death. I say "confirm" as in almost all cases the ICU doctors had already recorded in the chart their findings followed by "consistent with brain death." A second physician's opinion was needed to confirm brain death before life-support could be discontinued. Usually one of the attending physicians or residents-in-training gave me a brief history of how the one lying in front of me came to this point.

An ICU room has its own sounds and smells that over the years have embedded themselves in my memory. There is the rhythm of the respirator as the bellows push air into unwilling lungs at a fixed rate; in death all sense of "breathe in, breathe out" ceases as the brainstem no longer initiates respiration. The monitor above the bed presents a spectrum of multicolored lines representing the respiratory rate, heart rate, blood pressure, and oxygen saturation. More often than not, off to one side, standing or sitting as close as possible to the bed or crib, were parents and grandparents whose worn-out faces reflected the toll taken by keeping vigil for hours if not days. Their eyes were most often focused on that multicolored monitor as they watched for any variation that might either give them hope or prompt hope to fade, with the former much preferred.

Usually the families had already been told a neurologist was coming to do an examination that may or may not confirm brain death. Nonetheless, it was always just a bit awkward to introduce myself and explain what I was about to do. As a rule I never asked the family to leave the room during my exam, but I usually let them know that it was acceptable and understandable to do so.

As I bent over to look through widely dilated pupils, I nearly always caught a unique aroma that I had sensed so many times before. I cannot adequately describe it, but there is nothing else like it. I eventually came to think of it as the smell of death. It was always different from what I smelled in adult brain-dead patients. I sensed more of a sweet-but-not-sweet odor in children, but a quite unpleasant one in adults. It may have something to do with whatever it is that makes changing the diaper of a child quite different from changing the diaper of an adult. Perhaps that is why I hold the nursing assistant at the adult nursing home in such high regard as she does with ease what I find so difficult to do, but, when needed, I have done it anyway.

I usually told the family the "what" and the "why" for each step of my exam. It was my hope that they would not be alarmed. This approach did not always help allay fear and anxiety. I was about to do such things as touch their child's cornea with a wisp of cotton to see if there was any blink at all. Likewise, as a test of brainstem function, I was about to irrigate each ear in turn with cold water to see if the eyes would move in response. At some point I attempted to get the child's legs to move with some stimulation that would be painful for the conscious person. I usually pulled a blanket over the child's legs before stimu-lating a foot or leg, thereby shielding that act from the eyes of those who had already been afflicted by the sight of potentially painful acts being perpetrated on their child. When I checked deep tendon reflexes, such as a knee jerk reflex, I used either a small version of the Queen Square hammer or my giraffe reflex hammer. For the living the giraffe's nose hitting the patellar tendon brought some near-comic relief, albeit brief.

If an electroencephalogram (EEG) or cerebral blood flow studies had been done, I reviewed them before coming to the ICU. Then I would discuss those studies with the family. Families deserve as much explanation of these studies as they desire. Today, some families use an Internet search engine, such as Google, to find out enough to satisfy them. Not all such sites are created equal, so misinformation is readily available. Whatever the case, this is the time to answer questions.

One of the most frequently asked questions was in regard to an EEG that shows no activity. Brain electrical activity is usually recorded with scalp electrodes, not electrodes placed directly on the surface of brain or cerebral cortex. EEGs are done by trained technicians who prepare the scalp by cleaning areas where flat, round electrodes will be placed. As the recording is interpreted, consideration is given to factors that can lower the amplitude or height of brain waves. For example, barbiturates in high enough blood levels can bring about "flattening" of the brain waves. After significant brain injury, such as severe anoxia, pentobarbital- or benzodiazepine-induced coma may be used to reduce brain activity as much as possible, usually to a level of "burst-suppression" with alternating flat areas interrupted by brief bursts of activity. After a period of time, the medication is reduced, allowing the return of more brain activity. The aim is to minimize the damage done by the severe insult. Body temperature must be in a normal range at the time of the EEG as a cold body temp will decrease brain activity, leading to a false reading of "isoelectric" or "flat."

Even as a neurologist I saw something "priestly" in what I did. In some respects there was a ritual being followed as the steps in determining brain death had already been taken, and I now came to confirm what had been said and done. I then did my rituals of confirmation of the news that no one ever wanted to hear.

Now, years after I left medical practice, I was heading to the ICU to meet with the family of a man with a massive brain bleed. He had been declared brain-dead by the ICU physician, a finding confirmed by a neurologist. This time would be different from all other such journeys, for this time I would be there as a chaplain. Following the declaration of brain death, legally the ventilator could be stopped without asking the family first, for after all is said and done, dead is dead. However, the medical staff chose to meet with the spouse, children, and extended family to explain what brain death means. I, as a chaplain, stood silently observing the responses of family members and listening to the detailed explanation of what was about to happen.

Before the moment of brain death declaration, I already had some idea of who this man had been in life and how much he meant to those gathered.

By way of storytelling, he was no longer a stranger to me. We had gathered earlier to tell stories to honor this one who was unresponsive. Each in turn shared their fondest memories of his words, his facial expressions, his tools, and his hobbies. At such times the accuracy of stories matters little; what matters is reflecting on the best of what each family member and friend saw in the one now lying motionless except for the upheaving of his chest with each cycle of the respirator.

As a neurologist I had declared brain death more times than I can remember. There were children, some beaten to death; there were victims of meningitis, anoxic brain injury, and gunshot wounds to the head. The result for all was the same: no cerebral function as evidenced on standardized neurologic tests, electrocerebral silence on the EEG, and no bloodflow on a nuclear brain scan. There was not a great variation from declaration to declaration as brain death in and of itself always looks the same. On this day, however, something was different. Now I was looking at the brain-dead person and the family from the other side of the reflex hammer.

As I did during my medical career, I determined to stay with the family until the endotracheal tube was removed. As more family gathered, I became the messenger of what had been said or done already. As they encircled the bed, I stood behind the deceased's wife. I offered to pray and read a favorite scripture before extubation. I read Psalm 23, then led a prayer that most knew, the Lord's Prayer. Some were unsure of the words and varied them according to their memories of their last recitation. At such times, close enough is good enough.

After a time of tears and embraces, the family drew closer to the bed as life support was withdrawn. In reverent and almost priestly fashion, the nurse skillfully suctioned the endotracheal tube, deflated the balloon at the end of the tube that kept it from being readily dislodged, loosened its ties, and ever so gently slid it from his airway. The in-room heart monitor had been turned off so as to decrease the anxiety level of his family. Over the next few minutes cyanosis (turning blue) engulfed his face. Within a few minutes his heart stopped. The cries of those gathered intensified to sobbing; faces grew flushed; breathing rates increased; "he is gone; he is with God" filled the room. Recalling the responses of his family when told he was brain dead, it became clear to me that the finality of this man's life was not really appreciated until after the last breath was taken and the last heartbeat had faded into eternity. Now he was, in the minds of those who loved him, truly dead, not just "brain dead."

Cries continued to fill the room and tears flowed freely as, one by one, the moment seized the hearts of all. Then came the unexpected—it was my turn, as my eyes, blurred by tears, surveyed the room of modern medical equipment that could not prevent this moment, a moment we all must come to no matter what wonders modern medicine has to offer. It was the first time I had stood as the one who was supposed to offer spiritual comfort as needed, yet I was on the verge of being overwhelmed by it. I did not see that moment coming.

To an outside observer the scene may have been just like so many others in the ICU: family and friends gathering at life's end and nurses doing what nurses do. The passing observer knows neither what has transpired over the last several days nor the impact on those gathered, including on me. How often in my years in the practice of neurology had I been witness to such scenes without fully appreciating what was happening?

What I was experiencing was a moment of the ineffable. A powerful sense of something changing inwardly came over me. Here I was, sharing this space with fellow travelers I hardly knew, praying with them, and just being, not doing. Just being with those who are mourning is what I felt called to do at that moment. I was not there to be the diagnostician or consultant. I was not there to write an order in the chart, discuss treatment options, or do a procedure.

The space became more than just a hospital room; it had been transformed into sacred space into which I had been invited. For me, and I hope for others, this is a "thin space" where we glimpse God. The only proper response at such a time may well be silence. It is there in the silences of life that we are best able to hear God, even when God says nothing at all. God may be so silent that we, as did the Emmaus road travelers, fail to recognize the Presence. It may be days, weeks, even months later as grief has loosened its hold that we are able to say, "Surely the Lord was in that place."

Reflecting from this end of life on "peace" and how it has come to me along the way, I am prompted to wonder what events brought peace in the lives of those who have drawn their last breaths in my presence.

Peace in Open G

"She is at peace now," they said as they gathered around the Hill-Rom for the last time. Was it only now that she experienced freedom from disturbance? Did she not have other moments of peace?

As a child did she not crawl under the bed or slide in behind the overstuffed chair as the beer bottles and epithets flew?

Did she not in her earliest years have a canopy in the shrubs out back where only the birds knew of her presence and ceased their songs so she might hear silence?

Did she not have a childhood place near a dim light where she sat on a tub filled with soiled clothing and spread with a fading red blanket and there escape the bonds of immediacy?

Did she not have a carrel in a book-filled edifice where the only sounds were those of pages turning?

Did she not ever rock her grandchild and hum "You Are My Sunshine" until sleep came?

Did she not frequent a retreat where monks chanted the psalms in the pre-dawn hours?

Did she not ever hear Bach or Gounod on a 59 rank Austin organ or hear "Sanctus" in F major?

Did she not ever hear Scruggs' "Foggy Mountain Breakdown" or Bela's "Bach on a Banjo"?

Did she not ever find peace in five strings with open G tuning even if she was late on the chords and her fingers hurt with every G-C-D7-G?

I held her arthritic hands. I heard her story. We read the psalms.

In death she was not a stranger to peace.

Bill Holmes
November 2015

Note

[1]"Determination of death—Minimal conditions to be met," Kentucky Revised Statute 446.400, Kentucky Legislature, accessed August 31, 2017, http://www.lrc.ky.gov/statutes/statute.aspx?id=19420.

CHAPTER 3

"You Have Cancer"

I am focused on living with cancer, not dying from it. I choose as my metaphor "negotiating" with cancer, not battling it, as I know that there is great power in rapidly dividing cells. Cure may not come, but I will live or die as a whole person while giving thanks to the God of the resurrection.

Bill Holmes
Journal entry
February 7, 2010

In my lifetime I have been the messenger announcing the presence of cancer, the recipient of the cancer pronouncement, and the one who sits at the cancer patient's bedside as pastor/chaplain. I hope that what I share here will resonate with fellow travelers who have known cancer up close, sustained losses, or provided care in any capacity, including family member, nurse, nursing assistant, physician, or chaplain.

When Faith and Cancer Collide[1]

The thought of ever having cancer rarely crossed my mind ten years ago. In fact, looking back, I doubt I had ever seriously thought about the possibility of my own demise until I had heart surgery in 2002. Cancer did not loom large in my family history. My father had a low-grade prostate cancer, but no one else in my family had ever had cancer. My siblings have had cardiovascular disease or cerebrovascular problems, but for the most part my immediate family and close relatives have had to be innovative when it comes to finding a mode of dying.

Cancer usually comes uninvited, unwelcomed, and unexpected. My experience has been no different. In late 2009 my urologist told me I needed a transurethral prostatic resection (TURP). It was scheduled for early January. My wife and I arrived in the early morning hours with little or no apprehension about the procedure. After all, a TURP is common procedure. It was no surprise that all went well in the OR, at least as far as I knew. I was moved to post-op recovery where I slowly became aware of my surroundings—and my pain. I was later transferred to a semiprivate room. If you have ever been in such a room, then you know that "semiprivate" is a misnomer of the first order as there is absolutely no privacy. Your current medical problems cannot be easily kept from your roommate or his family. Within minutes I learned that the man next to me had just had surgery for colon cancer with metastatic lesions in the liver. He was very ill and in significant pain, but he was able to greet and welcome me to the room.

Shortly after I was settled in, my surgeon appeared in the doorway. His face was somber looking as he cleared his throat. He told me it was his habit to take a look in the bladder before doing the TURP. After all, the scope is already there, so why not get maximum benefit? Then came the words no one wants to hear: "Bill, you have bladder cancer that had not yet become symptomatic. Now, there is some good news in that I probably got all of it. We will do follow-up evaluation and see what happens."

I had not expected this—not at all. I was awake much of the night, processing what he had told me. The fact that he felt he had removed all of it offered little comfort initially. My name was now associated with *cancer*. It so happened that my self-pity was short-circuited by the suffering of my roommate, who moaned and cried out intermittently with pain. My job for that long night was to speak for him. I hit the call button more than a few times on his behalf, and morphine showed up in the room. Morning finally came, and I was discharged.

Two days later I was resting in bed in the late afternoon. The phone rang, and the caller ID showed my surgeon's name and number. He had the pathology report from the prostatic scrapings collected during surgery: "This is highly unusual. I did not expect it. Your PSA is good, but the pathologist read the slides as adenocarcinoma of the prostate, Gleason stage 6 to 7. We will confirm with a biopsy in three months." Dead silence ensued—from both ends of the call.

After thinking for a while about the news of two primary cancers, I disintegrated. One of the known uses for pillows is to muffle the sounds of being overwhelmed, complete with crying—no, make that wailing—and wondering out loud what was happening. I would give a verbatim, but some of my words might not be publishable. By day's end I was on the verge of making Job look like an amateur.

In brief, the bladder cancer has not returned, and I am still dealing with the prostate cancer. But there is "the rest of the story." For several decades my gastroenterologist has been removing multiple polyps from my colon every three years, as polyps have the potential to transform into cancer over time. In 2011 he found one in my mid-transverse colon, a favorite spot for cancer of the colon to appear. In medical school we were introduced to the "apple core sign," a radiographic finding created by the flow of contrast material being narrowed down by cancer and giving the appearance of an apple core sitting right in the middle of the transverse colon. It was the *sine qua non* for carcinoma of the colon. As it was, I did not need radiologic studies. The initial biopsy done by colonoscopy was negative for abnormal cells. However, because of the location of the polyp and my age at the time, the colorectal surgeon recommended colectomy with polypectomy. He felt I was going to be fine, but the location of the lesion dictated removal nonetheless.

The Robe[2]

My surgeon had a well-deserved vacation planned, and I wanted a well-rested surgeon probing the depths of my abdominal cavity. Besides, I had already been diagnosed with two primary cancers. What are the chances I would have a third? Eventually, the surgeon's office called with a date and time. My cardiologist sent a letter of permission to "anesthetize and surgically treat." Everything was set.

What now? I had lived in a hospital gown during the last hospitalization. This time I did not want to walk down the hospital corridor with my rear end showing through the open hospital gown that never fits and never ties completely shut. I last purchased a robe in July 2002 just before heart valve surgery. I live at night in lounge pants and a t-shirt. That is hard to do in the hospital where the medical team wants quick access to every part of your body.

It was off to the shopping mall to find a decent-looking robe. Macy's had only one in stock; it looked like one my grandfather wore. Sears had none that I would want to be caught dead in—and I intended to live! So on to the expensive place, Von Maur. Even the name causes my wallet to duck. A quick look in the men's clothing department, and there it was: navy blue with a thin white trim.

It cost more than I wanted to pay, but a check on my Amazon iPhone app told me it would not be cheaper online.

From behind me I heard, "May I help you?" The clerks in the men's department always look neatly dressed and professional. But this man's shirt looked to be a size too large and a bit loose around his neck but nonetheless neat. "Yes, I need a robe, and this one looks good to me," I said. His reply came softly as from one who was quite tired: "That one may be a little warm this time of the year." Almost without thinking I mumbled, "Not in the hospital."

That was his cue as he then told his story of just returning to work after two months in the hospital following surgery for colon cancer. The cancer had spread outside the colon: "They said they had done all they can do. They will scan me in six months. I came back to work this week." Then I understood the poorly fitting shirt. His thin neck, sallow complexion, and sunken eyes attested to the veracity of his cancer story. For the next ten minutes he told me more of his journey to date. It was *déjà vu* all over again, for I, as a physician, had heard that story hundreds of times, each with subtle differences. I nodded my head with some sense of understanding. Perhaps he was the reason I went robe shopping that day; perhaps he needed someone to hear his story, someone who could say, "Yes, I understand."

Finally, he asked me why I was going to the hospital. I felt like an imposter because I knew (at least I think I knew) that my problem had been caught early, and my shirts would probably fit in two months.

I keep the robe now hanging on my closet door to remind me of that day of a more than chance encounter with a fellow traveler who needed to tell his story. The robe was just the vehicle to move us both into a sacred space. I am again reminded that there is indeed a thin space where we glimpse God.

At least once every six months I drop by the store to see how the salesman is doing. We stand and chat for a few minutes. We had our picture made together in spring 2017. He is now over five years post-op and still going.

An Interesting Case

When I was a medical student, we learned many of our clinical skills by seeing patients on the wards and in the clinics. What any good student hoped for was a chance to do a history and physical on an "interesting" patient, which meant one who had a very full medical history and could, hopefully, articulate it. On the morning of my colon surgery, my surgeon asked if I was willing to be seen for pre-op evaluation by his junior medical student. After I answered in the affirmative, he turned to the student and said, "I think you will find Dr. Holmes to be an interesting case." Yes, heart valve surgery, prostate and bladder cancer, and a few other things make for an interesting patient. Possible colon cancer adds to the level of interest. I never really wanted to be an "interesting case."

The surgery went well. Post-op, I was not resting due to the noise level from nurses, medical students, surgery residents, and a ton of visitors. My doctor decided I would be better off at home. He was right. Twenty-four hours later my surgeon called me at home. I will never forget his words: "We made the right decision. The lesion we removed shows evidence of early cancer. The margins of the surgically removed tissue were clear of abnormal cells, and no lymph nodes were involved. We got it all."

How could this be? Three primary cancers within eighteen months? Despite this I was doing well and likely would continue to do so as long as I kept my follow-up visits for having my various body parts scoped—at least that is what I thought until June 2016. Over a period of five years since my last surgery, I had developed a sensory neuropathy with tingling, some numbness, and shooting pains in my feet. It felt like I was wearing heavy boots even when I had no shoes on at all. My doctor recommended some basic workup. I had multiple vials of blood drawn and left on vacation. Shortly after returning home I received a Friday afternoon call from my doctor informing me that my lab work was abnormal and I would need to see a hematologist. He had already set up an appointment for the following Tuesday.

A few weeks later I had a CT-guided bone marrow aspiration. As I was lying there on my abdomen and the radiologist was guiding the needle into my ilium, I could not help but think of the first bone marrow aspiration I had performed as a pediatric intern. My patient was a young girl whom we had sedated with chloral hydrate, a relatively old medication often used to induce sleep. Despite the sedation and generous numbing with xylocaine, she still moaned with pain as I placed the trocar in her ilium and aspirated marrow. She was diagnosed with acute lymphoblastic leukemia, a death sentence in 1971. As for me, I was given a diagnosis of "smoldering" multiple myeloma (MM); I would be around for a while yet.

I knew nothing about MM. It was not a pediatric disease. The next four nights I spent a lot of time on the National Library of Medicine website reviewing the world's literature. It is a disease of old people (fifty-five and above, more after sixty-five). There is a lot we don't know about it, but there is also a lot we do know. There is no cure, but there are ways to slow it down. I stayed up late reading several major review articles and many more research articles. I was in my default setting of intellectualizing and denial.

Over the next few weeks my days would give way to tears, self-pity, lament, and doubt. It was a period of uncertainty and not knowing. It was a time of what Walter Brueggemann refers to as my wait in the darkness and in disorientation, a waiting until "hell freezes over."[3]

The psalms of lament (e.g., 13, 35, 86) must have been written from the foxholes of life, from the OR recovery area, from the cancer ward, from the radiation therapy waiting room, from the oncologist's office, and from the bedside of a dying loved one. Brueggemann says the psalmist cries out to God because he is experiencing "disorientation."[4] And so do we.

In like manner we may also be so overwhelmed and frightened that we say, "Where is God? Has God abandoned me? Has God done a disappearing act just as the enemy, cancer, is at the door?" Being so "disoriented" that we question God is not something we readily claim. We tend to forget that our God is the God of the difficult times in our lives as well as the good.

It has been said that we Christians are unrelenting in our affirmation of "orientation," as reflected in our hymns and choruses. We seem to know where we are and where God is at all times. Such may come from the wishful optimism of our culture more than from faith in God.[5] Subsequently, when the threat of cancer arises, our faith, the foundation of our hope, is challenged, as we see the possibility of death. The reality of the threat of nonexistence, of no longer being here as a living, breathing person, stands in contradiction to our hope and even threatens our hope.

I was uncomfortable when I first considered the lament psalms as expressions of my own complaint to God about what I saw as the worst possible things happening to me. Was I not thankful for my life to this point? And who am I that I feel emboldened to, in a sense, get in God's face? It is, however, an act of faith to cry out in protest to God.[6] Our lament, our protest, and our outrage can potentially be the beginnings of a new journey through the darkest of times.

Like the writer of Psalm 13 we experience our wait in the darkness of death, our wait in disorientation, until we sense, hear, or feel a response from God.[7] I have a hard time fully describing what I felt as I sat in the darkness waiting to hear from someone other than my fearful and disoriented self. The response as perceived may not be the answer to all that is happening, but it can bring a time of new orientation in which, in faith, all of life is reconsidered and new priorities are set. In the midst of change and uncertainty, I found myself giving thanks and praising God that I have not yet been overcome by my enemy, cancer. Having heard "You have cancer," life is never again the same; a new ordering of life begins.

Not only the cancer sufferer but also the community of the cancer sufferer may become disoriented. There is upheaval in all areas of life. When the diagnosis comes, family and friends may rally around for a time, but as the treatment starts and the routine sets in, support may lessen. It is not out of lack of concern. Some may feel that they don't know what to say or do. In addition, there are times we tend to withdraw from community, as there is now a greater need for solitude and reflection. I found that I needed more time to think and pray and journal, things I could do only with some degree of solitude. I have come to the conclusion that there are times when we would do well as a community of faith—as family, caregivers, pastors, chaplains, and physicians—to carefully discern when it is time to be present and when it is best to take our leave.

We must be sensitive to individual spiritual needs as well as theological understandings that may not match ours. Above all, we must know that our well-intended sayings, even if they may reflect the truth of Scripture, carry the possibility of destroying faith and community. As I sat with the husband of a woman with a brain tumor, he informed me that he would have nothing to do with a religion that says "he is in a better place." Such were the words he heard from his pastor when his eight-year-old son died from leukemia twenty-five years earlier. "The place for my son was right here with his parents, not in some place called heaven," he said. He never returned to church.

Neither our faith and hope nor our being in a community of abiding faith and hope gives us a ticket to a cure, but it certainly helps us along the path to wholeness and healing when we face the disorientation of cancer. It is not surprising that the most requested song at our hospital is "Amazing Grace." It is song of being lost and found, of disorientation and coming to a new orientation.

Even those who cannot recite a theological definition of grace have come to know firsthand what grace means, as they have experienced horrible, inexplicable loss and fear followed by a strange inward assurance that somehow, in some mysterious way, God is touching their lives. Certainty about what is happening and why it is happening is not the issue. Even in the midst of recovery from surgery, the side effects of chemotherapy, the clinic and hospital visits, and the anguish of not knowing, we can and do find ourselves saying with the psalmist, "Where can I go from your spirit? Or where can I flee from your presence?... I come to the end—I am still with you" (Ps 139:7–8).

Living with the Unwanted

After the diagnosis of MM, several friends noted the change in my personality. Over the next few weeks I received emails, Facebook messages, and phone calls of concern. Eventually, I wrote the following in August 2016, sending it to friends and finally posting it on Facebook:

> Much has been written on coping and living with cancer or other potentially catastrophic illnesses. Nothing here will be original. Some of you have been where I am now, so you already know.
>
> I suppose we all handle things a little differently; there are no hard and fast rules for how we should respond. There are no commandments inherent in the universe to guide our gut-level responses. I say this despite a ton of literature that claims expertise of sorts, much of which is vicariously derived, or so it seems. As I read some treatises on grief, death, and dying, I am often moved to ask, "Has the author ever had cancer? How many bedsides has he/she attended? How many agonal breaths has he witnessed?"
>
> Meanwhile, if you see me in the hallway or at church or in the fitness center or at Walgreens (I think I am singlehandedly keeping them in business), you have my permission to talk about baseball, politics, theology, faith, pastoral care, medicine, or whatever comes to your mind other than multiple myeloma. I think about it enough already.
>
> I have been asked if I am going to this or that so-called center of excellence for multiple myeloma. Probably not, as there are no secrets

to the management of myeloma. All valid information is out there for all physicians and patients to see and read. Some centers do a research protocol from time to time, but most are for those who have failed the usual treatments. The one thing many "centers of excellence" are really good at is advertising.

In the past week or so I have shed more than a few tears. My lacrimal glands have not dried up; they are taking a rest so that I can see more clearly what needs to be done. Meanwhile, I will write, read, reflect, and continue living, as best I can, the life to which I have been called. As my one of my mentors often said, "Sometimes our best is none too good." My checkered life, filled with missteps, uncertainties, and failures mixed with intermittent success, will no doubt remain that way.

Here some may ask, "What about prayer? You did not mention prayer." I say, "What do you think you have been reading? I believe we should live our lives as a prayer. All we say or do in this life begins with "Our Father" and ends with "Amen."

A Final Thought

Some people hear that they have cancer, and then in a matter of months or a few years, they are gone from us. Others have a long history of remission and relapse; they often defy the statistics. We all know one or more who have died from cancer despite doing all the "right" things and undergoing all the modern therapies. I am often amazed when I sit in front of cancer patients and hear their stories with all the ups and downs, complete with horrible pain and suffering. I am not sure what words might work best to describe them, but I offer these: courageous, introspective, inspiring, most often gracious, and without self-pity. How many times have I visited a cancer patient with the hope that I might be a help and a blessing, and then I depart feeling renewed, encouraged, and blessed?

I have been asked on more than one occasion to comment on how I feel now about having four primary cancers but continuing to do well. I have never needed radical surgery; I have never had chemotherapy. I get up early to write, work in the flower garden, and then do the work of a chaplain. As one friend put it, "Bill, you don't look like a cancer sufferer." All of this raises the question of how I feel as I see longtime friends succumb to cancer while I am still here and doing well. I sit in the waiting room of my oncologist's office and see in some the ravages of cancer and the side effects of chemotherapy, but I have had none of this.

All of my cancers have been found early. This is not just luck or good fortune. First of all, I have what I call the "Three Ws"—I am white, wealthy, and well insured. If I were black, I would have less access to wealth and healthcare. I would be less likely to have access to early cancer detection.

Without going into detail here, I am compelled to insert a word about our healthcare system. We have great disparities in our system with income and race playing a major role. Even as I write, the U.S. Senate is embroiled in a battle to "repeal and replace" so-called "Obamacare." It is more about politics than finding a way to ensure healthcare for all Americans. Much has been written on this subject. I have listed a few excellent books at the end of this chapter.[8]

So how do I feel? At times I want to say that it is ridiculous and unfair that one person should have an early diagnosis of four primacy cancers and walk away almost unscathed while a myriad of cancer sufferers struggle to stay alive or succumb to the onslaught of malignancy. I have no way of knowing how long MM had been smoldering away in my body, nor would knowing make a great deal of difference now, as there is no cure. So what can I say? I am rarely speechless, but the last few years I have had no adequate words. Resisting any temptation to claim a special blessing or dispensation from God, I linger in the shadow of uncertainty cast by cancer. Meanwhile, I am filled with awe and gratitude. How can this be? I don't know. It just is. Amen.

To Life

A few days after I was diagnosed with MM, I was sitting on the steps looking at the flowers, shrubs, and trees I had planted over the course of thirty-six years. Wild rabbits chased after the unseen, and squirrels were playing in the cypress trees. I leaned back on the deck and wrote what follows.

I told the deer to help themselves
to the delicate branches of the weeping cherry

I told the wild rabbits to nibble
on the now-sparse lilies

I told the raccoons they could raid
the garbage cans and play on the deck

I told a robin she could make her nest
in the bend of the freshly painted gutter

I told the chipmunks they could dig holes
in my flower garden and under the shrubs

I told the squirrels they could build nests
on any desired branch of the gum tree

I told the bees to help themselves to the nectar
of flowers of every hue in the garden

I told them all to go ahead
if that is what they needed to survive

From the burning bushes to the white pine
and along the creekside lined with cypress

From the tulip poplar to the mountain fire
and through the jungle of caladiums

From the sweetbay magnolia
And through the dense vinca

Hearts beat on and on…
and the backyard is full of life

Bill Holmes
August 2016

Notes

[1] Bill Holmes, "When Faith and Cancer Collide," Church Health Reader, accessed August 31, 2017, http://chreader.org/faith-cancer-collide/. Used with permission.

[2] Bill Holmes, "The Robe," *Church Health Reader* 3, no. 3 (Fall 2013): 9. Used with permission.

[3] Walter Brueggemann, *The Message of Psalms: A Theological Commentary* (Minneapolis: Augsburg, 1984), 59–60.

[4] Ibid.

[5] Ibid., 51.

[6] Ibid., 52.

[7] Ibid.

[8] The following books are recommended: Elisabeth Rosenthal, *An American Sickness: How Healthcare Became Big Business and How You Can Take It Back* (New York: Penguin Press, 2017); Eric Topol, *The Patient Will See You Now: The Future of Medicine Is in Your Hands* (New York: Basic Books, 2016).

CHAPTER 4

Community

Community is something I have not done well. So, you might ask, why I am offering my thoughts on the subject. First and foremost, in community I have had my greatest sense of the presence of God. It is in community that God does what God does. A community is not just a collection of people gathered around us, but a group with a common bond. We have a natural bond in our family of origin even though it sometimes is fractured by life experiences. But community arises out of our shared life experiences that come to all of us in some way and at some time. These include, of course, illness and suffering. The cause and the mode of our illnesses and disabilities have the potential to disenfranchise us and leave us outside our identity group. Consider also the impact of aging that often brings with it dementia and loss of mobility with greater dependence on others and a loss of community. Dying in community is not an oft-considered topic, but my experiences of the last few years suggest that we as a society often fail the dying as they draw their last breath alone. Finally, we have allowed technology to either distort or redefine how we relate to each other. It is with all of these in mind that I share my thoughts on community.

Arriving mid-morning in the ICU to check on a ninety-year-old man, I noticed his nurse was not one I had ever met. I introduced myself and soon learned that she was usually gone by 7:30, as she worked the night shift. I assumed someone had not shown up for work so she had stayed to help. I quickly learned my assumption was incorrect. Over the last several nights she had come to know this man who was likely to die soon. She was concerned he was going to die without friends or family with him. To date there had been no visitors. She decided to stay, as his death was imminent. His life-support system had been withdrawn, and intravenous fluids had been stopped. A "do not resuscitate" order had been written for him in keeping with his advance directive executed several months before. The nurse I had just met was at his bedside holding his hand as he took his last breath and passed into eternity.

Not infrequently, someone dies in a hospital room without the presence of family or friends. In some cases it is because the one dying is quite elderly and his friends and family are deceased, in poor health, or simply unable to withstand keeping a death vigil. In other instances the one taking his last breath apparently had not seen building community as important. He may have had acquaintance and some he counted as friends but had few or none with whom he had built close relationships. In most instances we do not know why there is an apparent lack of community. I can only venture an educated guess by looking at my own adventures and misadventures in building community.

Although I am not an expert on the subject of community, there are a few things I have learned through my own experiences. As strange or contradictory as it may sound, I believe community begins in solitude. By solitude I do not mean just being alone. As most who might read this already know, you can be lonely while seated in a crowded room. In fact, there are those who say they can find solitude in a coffee shop. I quite agree that solitude is not necessarily a state of being alone or in total quietness. Wherever we find solitude, we need to go there as often as our soul requires it. As for me, I need the type of solitude that I find in the early morning hours when there are no TVs on, no phones ringing, and as few distractions as possible. It is then I can hear my inner self and listen for God to somehow speak out of the silence. And yes, I do have a hard time distinguishing between God's voice and my own. Nonetheless, it is during those times of solitude that my noisy heart is quiet enough to hear beyond itself.

My mother was nearly deaf most of her life. Though she wore hearing aids, the technology of the time did not make the spoken word more understandable. Even then, when my three siblings and I were noisy beyond belief, she would demand that we tone things down so she could "hear [herself] think." Perhaps that is what we all need—a time when things are toned down so we can hear ourselves think—and maybe, just maybe, God will get a word in as well. Given a chance, God turns our attention to others and their needs. Out of our solitude come community and service to others.

We cannot truly build community without first investing ourselves in the lives of others. It is not an easy thing to do, for we must first get up from our chairs and leave our virtual communities, at least for a while. We must pay attention to who people are. We do not have to "figure them out," but we do need to come to a point of appreciation of their unique life stories.

Of People and Puzzles

I like working puzzles. I keep one going almost all the time. The more difficult they are, the more enjoyable they are. I think, reflect, and even pray every now and then in between the "Eureka!" and "Doggone, where in the world does this belong?"

When I first look at a puzzle, I do not immediately appreciate all the subtleties of color, hue, lines, and other clues to where this or that piece belongs. This is particularly true of paintings by famous artists such as Van Gogh. Over time subtle variations break into my awareness so that a puzzle piece sitting off to the side suddenly jumps up and says exactly where it fits. Eureka!

Invariably, there is a piece that I cannot figure out where it belongs until the very end. It is as if Van Gogh knew that one day someone would make a puzzle out of one of his masterpieces, so with a slight twist or flip of the brush he would put in something that does not fit my mind's take on reality, on what an iris or a sunflower should look like. Thank God for artists, for they know how to reinterpret the world!

Recently, I took some of my puzzles to a retirement center where puzzle working is a social event. One woman volunteered her philosophy on and love for puzzles: "They are like people; they have to be figured out and the pieces put together." I smiled and nodded in agreement; however, before I reached my pickup truck, I had recanted.

When I first look at a puzzle, with all of its parts spread out over a table, I do not immediately have an idea of what the assembled parts will look like. Yes, there is a picture on the box, but the finished puzzle almost never looks exactly like the box picture. Over time a picture of the puzzle as a finished product slowly evolves in my mind. When I first meet another person, I do not immediately and fully see the one in front of me. Over time the unclear becomes a little clearer as some things about the other might become more understandable. What I later see might or might not support my first take. But this puzzle metaphor doesn't go much further. We are not puzzles to be figured out and put together. When I get up each morning and look at a puzzle spread out all over the table, I find all of the parts look just as I left them. They have no potential to change, not one iota. The variously shaped pieces will not morph into something else; they are what they are. However, over time we do change, even if only in subtle ways. We are more like a piece of art that is to be beheld and appreciated.

Our perspective over time changes how we see the same piece of art. Rembrandt would not have been pleased to hear that years ago I could look through all of his great works in record time. However, today I can sit before a Rembrandt for hours and see a good deal more than yesterday. A reproduction of Rembrandt's interpretation of the return of the prodigal son hangs in front and to the right of my desk. Over the last twenty-five years I have seen different stories in the same painting as I consider the perspectives of the father, the son, and the older brother.

Unless we are already dead, then who we are today is not necessarily who we will be tomorrow. Our human tendency is to assume we already know all there is to know of the other. In making that assumption we turn the other into a finished work, frozen in time. However, I think we are forever being changed and renewed, even though we might look the same at first glance. Of necessity we must linger longer before the masterpiece, the person now sitting before us, and come to know that person again and again and again. Let us hope we will have the grace to do so, for that is where we will find community.

A Community Unaware

I told her I would be at the nursing home in time for lunch. Being on time was not my greatest concern; it was just having the wherewithal to be there at all. I did not always want to go. Why? Perhaps I feared too much that which must inevitably come.

I signed in at the desk as I always do, put on my visitor's sticker, and started down the hallway. I paused in front of the elevators to greet an old friend moving slowly along on his walker. The opening of the elevator gave me a momentary reprieve from looking at what my future might hold. I pushed the button for the second floor, and within seconds the door was opening again. I turned left and went past the sitting area and then past the room where fifteen years ago my father had taken his last breath.

Finally, I came to the nurses' station where a dozen gray heads, mostly women, all in wheelchairs and all in various states of alertness, were now assembled. Here was this gathering that perhaps in another day may have been sitting around the courthouse or the local beauty shop telling stories as they observed all that was going on in the immediate community.

As soon I opened my mouth to greet my aunt, many of those gathered flinched ever so slightly and raised their heads briefly. Some even verbalized a weak "hello." I don't think she even knew I was there until I spoke. Macular degeneration had long ago stolen all but her peripheral vision. But nothing had laid claim to her hearing. Unlike her sister, my mother, she could hear the proverbial pin drop.

The closer I came to the circle, the more activity there was among those who were at one time slumbering in their chairs. It was as if they anticipated a visitor, and even though I was not necessarily there to see them, it was an occasion for excitement of a sort.

I am reminded of long-ago trips to the kennel to pick up our dog. Upon our arrival she would start to jump and bark in anticipation of being freed from her temporary captivity. Then the entire K-9 community would join in with barks and yelps and jumps. I often wondered if they thought I was going to take them as well. Were they celebrating the release of their friend, or were they asking to go with her?

I am not saying this gathered community of the elderly was a gathering of pets. In fact, each time I went, I found myself looking for a way to say to their caregivers, "I know this man; I know that woman. In fact, I have known her for a long time. Let me tell you what she has done with her life." There are several in the community I've known for well over a half century. I knew them when they were very active in our church, perhaps as teachers and deacons. I could easily catalog all of their accomplishments. This man, for instance, was an accomplished attorney who did more than his share of *pro bono* work. He was a quiet man, but when he spoke, his words were full of wisdom. Then one day Parkinson's disease took over his life. And this woman, the one slumped over in her chair and seemingly unaware of anything, was a key voice in the choir every Sunday. I did not need to use my eyes to see if she was present on any given Sunday; my ears would suffice. So this was not a gathering of a generic bunch of nobodies; rather, it was an assembly of people with their own unique stories to be heard, shared, and honored.

Because the one I went to visit was among the most alert and verbal of all, my aunt also received the most attention from the staff, or so it seemed. She had stories to tell, plenty of them. She had survived the great depression, the great flood of 1937, and the loss of five siblings and her husband. She had birthed no children, but she was not childless, for she had essentially adopted her seven nieces and nephews.

From time to time, with just a little prompting, she would tell stories of working for Curtis Wright aircraft during World War II as a "Rosie the Riveter." She would tell stories of being a "bucker" who would climb inside the aircraft and hold a metal plate on one side of a rivet hole while on the outside another woman would pound a hot rivet in place. By day's end she was very hot, sweaty, and exhausted. She did not recall the pay, except that it was not very much. She always quickly added, "But in those days nobody made very much, but it was enough."

The dining room is down a long corridor. She liked to use her legs to propel her wheelchair, but on the days I visited, she asked me to push her along. We passed the nurses' station, then room after room bearing the names of many of those gathered in the hall awaiting assistance for the journey. The dining room is set up as a series of tables that hold from two to eight. Many know their places for the meal. Not being where you belong is cause for an immediate response by one or more. That response might be simply a coming to attention while still seated or perhaps a sudden change in the degree of eye opening. While being out of place causes distress for some, not being there at all prompts great concern from the many. That concern may not be verbalized, but it can be seen in searching eye movements and brief but distinct body shifts. A spot at the table being unoccupied several meals in a row might bring greater agitation initially, but then comes a look of knowing. Perhaps they know without being told that, indeed, something has happened to claim a part of the community. The more verbal members of this community will dare ask one of the attendants. The sharing of medical information is not allowed, but the verbal presentation of an obituary is permissible. "She has passed" may be the only thing said, leaving it to the rest of the community to figure out what happened, to discern what they already knew.

My aunt, more often than not, would go immediately after the meal to a room where she last recalled seeing the presumed deceased. Confirmation is always needed. Seeing the bed empty is not met with tears but only a blank look out into the distance. From time to time she reiterated her desire to move on, to be gone. How often did I hear her ask, "Is this where I will live until I die?" And I would say, "If you would like to live elsewhere, you can." Several times she countered, "No, I like it here. They treat the prisoners well." Such was her humor.

Like so many others at the nursing home, my aunt tended to "sundown," meaning she made more sense in the morning than in the evening. In the morning she was occasionally philosophical. Not long ago as we sat talking on a Saturday morning, she observed the irony of starting life and ending life in diapers. She observed that, unlike the diapers of her childhood, the ones she wore now could be thrown away. She lamented the fact that her mother had to soak and wash the old cloth diapers. "I suppose that is why she ended up working in a laundry, the old Limerick Laundry," she dryly remarked. And so the visit went until sleep intervened.

Elizabeth Francis Herod, "Aunt Fran," went to live elsewhere the day after Easter 2017. According to her nurse her last words were, "I suppose this is the day I will see my mother again."

Chronic Neurologic Conditions and the Church

And when was it that we saw you sick or in prison or neurologically or cognitively impaired or autistic or epileptic or...? "And the King will answer them, saying, 'Truly I tell you, just as you did it to one of the least who are members of family, you did it to me'" (Matt 25:40).

Alex had intractable epilepsy and cerebral palsy with autistic features. He died in his sleep at age seven. In the early morning hours I went to the ER to be with Alex and his family. Shortly after my arrival the chaplain asked the family if she could call their pastor. Alex's mother replied, "Pastor? Church? No church would have us. We were told that our child was a disturbance with his crying out and intermittent seizures. Some would glare at us when we rolled Alex's wheelchair into worship. Invariably the usher would embarrass us by asking us to move to the vestibule. Church? Call no church for us!"

Unfortunately, this story is a recurring one in churches today. Both adults and children with debilitating neurologic conditions, as well as their families, might experience difficulty finding a place in the church. The scope of the problem is often unrecognized. For example, children and teens with autism spectrum disorders often face difficulty finding a place. Churches are doing better with wheelchair ramps, but most often they provide an area for wheelchairs only at the back of the sanctuary, almost never at or near the front. Perhaps this is reflective of how our society in general sees people with disabilities.

Despite the passage of the Americans with Disabilities Act in 1990, our culture, including churches, has not been diligent in going the extra mile to be welcoming. This happens against a background of living in a nation that still is one of the few having no national healthcare system or single-payer system. Children with disabilities often have significant unmet medical needs due to lack of availability or access. Adults and children with all sorts of disabilities are also more likely to live at or below the federally established poverty line. A few years ago it was estimated that one-third of persons with disabilities were in poverty. That estimate certainly meets my experience over the last twenty-five to thirty years.

When I was medical director of the Kentucky Commission for Children with Special Health Care Needs in the 1990s, I helped establish tertiary medical care delivery points in the central and western half of the state. UK had been doing the same in Appalachia since the 1970s. I started pediatric neurology clinics in Owensboro, Bowling Green, and Elizabethtown, thereby hopefully making it easier for families to access the needed care. The nurses and social worker in the clinics were superb at getting to know the needs of our families. Stories of feeling rejected by the local church were not infrequent.

Not long ago I sat at the bedside of a woman who was quite ill with kidney failure. Upon noting "pastoral care" on my identification badge, Margaret asked about my church affiliation. I explained to her that I do have a church membership, but I tend to leave that identity at the door. I am there for any person from any church or no church. She immediately replied, "No church? That is my church—no church." Then she told her story.

She was the second of four children. Her older brother, Roy, had severe cerebral palsy and epilepsy. He was, of course, nonverbal, making only intermittent loud noises that were not necessarily related to discernable discomfort. At times he cried out for several hours as he sat in his wheelchair. When the family started attending a local church, several members objected to Roy's noisy presence. One Sunday afternoon the pastor and a few deacons showed up at Roy and Margaret's home and announced that they were there to pray over Roy. As Margaret recalls, they said Roy was "prayer matter." As "prayer matter" they would visit periodically and pray over him, but they preferred that the family not bring him to church. The entire church was apparently in agreement.

Margaret never returned to church. Roy died two years later in a nursing home.

Even as the church seeks to define itself as inclusive, many with disabilities have neither a real place in the church nor ministry geared for them. Others object to anything that might interrupt an otherwise quiet and orderly worship service. At the same time we build fine buildings, or we argue over who shall receive Communion or whose baptism counts, issues that have little to do with those trying to survive in the world.

Chronic neurologic disease, especially in children, can present with complex problems. A child with cerebral palsy may also have epilepsy, learning disabilities or mental retardation, and secondary behavior problems. There is also poverty and lack of employment opportunities for parents, as they must stay home to care for the disabled child. The parents' problems are further compounded by self-blame, depression, an increased divorce rate, and prolonged grief over the loss of the hoped-for child who can never be.

Among all with disabilities, the single characteristic many find in common at one point in their lives is *isolation*. Their conditions isolate them through immobility, unemployment, inadequate education or training, housing unsuitable to their abilities, poverty, and, all too frequently, lack of adequate healthcare. Unfortunately, the church sometimes adds to this isolation by failure to appreciate or respond adequately to special needs. Mainstreaming, seen as a model in schools, is often not well received in the church.

There are those churches that seem to know how to reach out and be inclusive. Not long ago my home church, HBC in Louisville, had a youth-led worship service. Among those leading us were a young lady with Down syndrome and a young man who had survived a brain tumor but had been left with speech and walking difficulty. This is church as it should be.

There is biblical basis for reaching out to include those who are disabled or "*otherwise-abled.*" Jesus seemed to go out of his way to meet the needs of neurologically impaired folks: the man born lame, the child with epilepsy, and the withered hand. In the first century the good religious folks for the most part ignored such needs or, even worse, blamed the problems on sin, even the sins of the parents. The biblical narrative offers examples of love and concern for those marginalized due to their neurologic or medical conditions. There were those who carried the paralyzed man on a bed to Jesus (Matt 9:2) and those who "brought to him a deaf man" (Mark 7:32). A father brought his epileptic son (Luke 9:38). The lepers came on their own, as they, considered contagious and ritually unclean, had little or no community (Mark 1:40–45).

New Testament scholar Jaime Clark-Soles offers a new perspective on the old story of Lazarus as recorded in John 11. She raises the question of what killed Lazarus. Noting the use of the imperfect verb in John 11:1, "Now a certain man was ill," Clark-Soles speculates about the possibility that Lazarus had a chronic condition. Those gathered to mourn asked a question that might well be raised by those who know and care for persons with disabilities today. They wanted to know if something could be done to make his lot in life better.[1]

Clark-Soles goes on beautifully to raise a question for all of us, especially the church. Do we as a community have the wherewithal, the tenacity, to keep trying to enable Lazarus, not just for a while but until his life is truly over? Will we be a community that enables or disables? While it is Jesus who cures, it is the community that has the power to enable.[2]

The faith community can be of extreme importance in the lives of those with chronic neurologic condition and their families. Failure to include them can be devastating, as in the case of Alex and his parents. The challenge to the church is to create the conditions that will support and maintain the spiritual life of individuals with disabilities and their families. Such cannot wait until the need shows up at the door but must take shape through long-term planning for space, teachers, programs, and workers. This means the budget must also reflect the concern. Someone should be designated as "minister to those differently abled." A team should be assembled proactively that includes those with disabilities, their families, the parish nurse, other health professionals in the church, and special education teachers.

The question for us: "Will we enable Lazarus, or will we perpetuate his disability?"

A Community of Compassion, Not Judgment

In the halls of medicine or in the pews of the church, the announcement that a person has this illness or that might evoke moral judgment statements. Hearing that a man has just been diagnosed with lung cancer, some will ask, "Well, was he a smoker?" An overweight woman suffers a heart attack and we hear, "If she had lost weight, then this would not have happened."

In the early 1980s I rendered care to a man complaining of headaches, weight loss, and extreme malaise. A CT brain scan revealed an unusual lesion. At the time we had no MRI available in Louisville. Arrangements were made for my patient to go to Vanderbilt University in Nashville for an MRI of his brain. The neuroradiologist interpreted the scan as showing inflammation in the right parietal lobe. Brain biopsy was performed on that area. Our pathologists were uncertain about what they were seeing. The biopsy material was sent to the UK neuropathology department. Late the next evening the UK pathologist called me at home. He saw evidence of a retrovirus with additional evidence of toxoplasmosis. The most likely diagnosis: CNS HIV-AIDS, meaning central nervous system infection with HIV with secondary toxoplasmosis. I had never seen this entity. The first reported cases of AIDS in the United States were published in 1981; all reported cases were in white male homosexuals according to the CDC.[3]

Despite being treated by the standards of the day, he worsened to the point of needing a nursing home. No facility could be found that understood the disease enough to take him. He was placed in an isolation room at a local hospital.

"Isolation room" was an appropriate label in several ways. The hospital's intent was primarily to prevent the passage of pathogens in or out of the room. In my patient's case there was also isolation from community, family, and the church. He was more than isolated; he was, in essence, abandoned because of his diagnosis and his sexual orientation.

Four months later he died in a hospital isolation room with his life partner, a nurse, and me present. No other family or friends were there. No one came from his church where he had been an active and giving member until his illness. It was 6 a.m. on New Year's Day.

Let us agree for the moment that we *do* have habits and lifestyles that contribute to our poor health and the shortening of our lives. However, when a person arrives at the hospital or clinic with serious or life-threatening medical problems, our concern for what got them there is coming after the fact. Our proper response should be to exercise compassion and help that person live in the now. Often the effects of judgment by family, friends, and caregivers are as bad as the disease process itself. Given time and permission, it is not unusual for patients to express a sense of guilt for their medical problems. Jesus did not speak of bad decisions and risky behaviors to those who came to him for healing. It was the religious leaders who were concerned about assigning fault.

For the first-century Mediterranean person, an illness or disease was anything that separated them from community. Social isolation came as a result of having a certain set of signs and symptoms that the community interpreted as unacceptable, unclean, or impure. The sick and the lame thus came seeking restoration to society, even as the religious authorities raised the issue of assigning fault.

Jesus got into trouble for healing and befriending those whom society had marginalized. Thus, he was placed into conflict with the religious and civil leaders. First of all, Jesus had the power from God to heal, but the powers-that-be did not grant him that authority. Secondly, his actions challenged the systemic order that said, "If you have these signs or these symptoms, then you are out of the community. You have no claim to compassion, community, and healing."

In John 9:2 the question is raised as to whose sin had caused a man to be born blind, the man or his parents. Jesus said it was neither, but that the power of God may be made manifest. Jesus did not go looking to assign causation or blame for the man's blindness, but he did see it as an occasion for doing God's work of healing. An encounter with one facing loss of health should be an occasion for compassion and offering of community, not pronouncing judgment, whether it be overtly or subtly.

The Techno Age and the Absence of Presence[4]

She had just been told she had metastatic cancer. At the oncologist's request and with her permission, I pulled up a chair, sat down, and leaned in to hear her story. I was introduced to six family members who sat quietly around the room. As she was talking, only two of her family appeared to be listening to what she had to say. The other four were staring at their smartphones; they were either tuning in to Facebook, checking emails, or texting. At her hour of greatest need, some of her family was in cyberspace, a virtual world, or, ironically, on a "social network." Their bodies were in the room, but their attention was elsewhere; they were not truly present to their loved one. There was, indeed, an absence of presence.

In his award-winning book *On Presence*, Ralph Harper charges that we seem to have lost any real sense of what it means to be present to each other.[5] I see presence as not only our bodies being in spatial relationship to each other, but also as a full awareness of what is happening and being said, both verbally and nonverbally. Presence is experienced by all the senses. We see each other with all our wrinkles and scars; we hear each other with all our intonations and nuances; we touch each other with a touch we have hopefully known before or will know again; even our sense of smell might identify significant people in our lives before we see or hear them.

In our age of "virtual" everything, our sense of presence to each other and to God has diminished. Sherry Turkle observes that technology has offered us a substitute for face-to-face connection. And we have bought into it as we have let technology redefine the boundaries between intimacy and solitude. Rather than investing our selves in others, rather than getting to know each other face-to-face, we build a list of Facebook friends and then are left to wonder if they are really friends and what that means. As we develop our online identity and avoid real-time happenings, as they take "too much time," we may find ourselves feeling utterly alone.[6] Knowing each other and God intimately takes investment of time and our selves.

At a chaplains' conference the virtues of technology were extolled as a means of spiritual presence. A good deal of excitement and affirmation was voiced for what I call "techno-spirituality." While I see the possibilities offered by new technology, I fear we will be fooled into believing we are fully present to one another. Why must we feel more at home or comfortable with a virtual presence than a real presence? Is it because we are not capable of giving our selves completely, an act that cannot be done in virtual space or cyberspace but requires what Buber called "the real filled present"?

Social media offers some good, such as keeping in touch with old friends and family in distant places. For those confined by health or other circumstances, Facebook can be at least some level of connection. And who does not want to see pictures of grandchildren or use FaceTime to chat with them? Texting clearly has value as a means of rapid communication and can be life-saving in emergencies but life-taking when done while driving. But we have become preoccupied with such technologies, allowing them to become a poor substitute for real presence, for face-to-face encounters.

We are in a sense becoming "digitally disembodied."[7] Observe any public event and you will find a substantial number of people are on their smartphones as the ballgame or the lecture or, yes, even worship happens. Ironically, in the age of Facebook, we are in danger of losing face-to-face presence. How do we come to know and understand the mystery of the other without real or actual presence? If we must do our technological communication *ad nauseum*, then let us never fool ourselves into believing we are present to the other in our entirety, with our whole being.

We risk remaining strangers to one another. We fail to give our selves to each other by sitting face-to-face and listening in a life-giving manner. We keep our selves for our selves as we hit send or post. To leave cyberspace for real presence is to give our selves without the fear that we will have nothing left if we do.

We cannot afford to be dismissive or take lightly that which is communicated by a grasped hand, a breathing pattern, an intonation, a look, and the ineffable experience of just being there. It is during the face-to-face encounter with our iPhones turned off that we find real presence rather than loneliness and even darkness. As chaplains or pastors our presence in and of itself has the potential to be a healing balm. Words are not necessarily needed. When I was in pediatric training, one of my mentors had a sign above his desk that read, "Don't just do something. Stand there!" To this admonition we might add, "Don't just say something. Be there!"

Why do I hold these concerns? Why am I so convinced? I have been both the one holding the smartphone and the one who experienced the absence of presence when real presence was direly needed.

Finally, consider this: All that we do in this life can be seen as an act of community, even our very work. At the end of every worship service at HBC, my pastor, Joe Phelps, reminds us that we leave that place to go out into the world to do our true acts of worship, which is our very lives. I am reminded of William Stringfellow's assertion that our work is worship, as he defines worship as the sum of all that we do.[8] Our work is an offertory. Moreover, work as worship/witness is not done as a solitary act, but offered in community; therefore, we must offer it in the community of faith as it gathers for corporate worship. It is as though our entire being is something to be offered in community. Amen.

Notes

[1] Jaime Clark-Soles, *Reading John for Dear Life: A Spiritual Walk with the Fourth Gospel* (Louisville: Westminster John Knox Press, 2016), 78.

[2] Ibid.

[3] "First Report of AIDS," MMWR Weekly, June 1, 2001, CDC, accessed August 31, 2017, www.cdc.gov/mmwr/preview/mmwrhtml/mm5021a1.htm.

[4] Bill Holmes, "Virtual Community? The Absence of Presence," *Word and World* 35, no. 2 (Spring 2015): 183–85. Used with permission.

[5] Ralph Harper, *On Presence: Variations and Reflections* (Philadelphia: Trinity Press International), 1.

[6] Sherry Turkle, *Alone Together: Why We Expect More from Technology and Less from Each Other* (New York: Basic Books, 2012), 189.

[7] The origin of this term is unknown to the author.

[8] William Stringfellow, *Instead of Death: New and Expanded Version* (Eugene: Wipf and Stock, 2004), 69.

CHAPTER 5

What about Heaven?

During a lunchtime escape to a local bookstore, I noticed three of the nonfiction top-ten bestsellers were books on heaven. Eben Alexander's *Proof of Heaven* had the top spot.[1] Why so much on heaven, particularly in a secular context? Surely the books resonated with someone. Returning to the hospital, I asked some of our staff if they were familiar with these books. They were more than familiar; they were conversant, reciting passages and ideas from Alexander's book as well as Todd Burpo's *Heaven Is for Real.*

From my conversations with patients, nurses, and Eucharistic ministers, I find that heaven, or the afterlife in general, may be one the most significant but undiscussed, even avoided, topics inside and outside the walls of either the hospital or the church.

Do a Google search for heaven, and you will find more than a half-billion results. Courses, books, essays, and artist impressions abound. The same holds for near-death experiences (NDEs). You can take a two-week course on NDEs for $1,500. There is a reason the Internet is full of such: people want to know. Many of the sites seek to answer the following questions: How do I get to heaven? What does heaven look like? Some offer "proof of heaven" arguments. The source of knowledge does not seem to be all that important to many. The experiences of a neurosurgeon, a child as reported by his father, or the views of a journalist will all suffice.

References to heaven, generally thought of in Christianity as the place of God's presence beyond the confines of earth, are commonly overheard at wakes and funerals. Some report that in the hallways of medicine such references are infrequent. As a physician-turned-chaplain, I am attuned to talk of death and dying and, yes, even afterlife. Simply listening to critically ill patients and their families long enough often yields some reference to what will happen after death. Even in their silence, I suspect others are thinking about what will happen to their souls after death, or if indeed there is an "after." Still others seem to need permission to even speak or ask questions about death and afterlife, as they fear it will be taken as sign of "giving up" and not "battling" their illness. As one dying woman put it, "I fear to talk openly about my doubts about anything that even sounds like afterlife. In my family such would be considered a total faith failure."

Shortly after my bookstore visit, I encountered a tearful woman whose husband of fifty-six years was dying after a prolonged illness. She accepted that death was at hand. She asked on several occasions, "What about heaven? Will I see my husband again in heaven?" Her son, seemingly embarrassed by the question, interrupted her: "Of course, Mom, of course." She had asked the same questions of her pastor. Had he addressed her questions? She said, "He came in, said a brief prayer, shook all our hands, and said he would see us later." She felt the pastor acted as if he did not hear the question. Her question has stayed with me. Initially, I heard only the concern about the nature and/or existence of heaven. Over time I heard the other part of the question, or perhaps the real question: "Will I see my husband again?" In any case, who does hear the questions? Where do people go to find answers about death, afterlife, heaven, and "Will I see him again?"? The pastor/chaplain should also be cognizant of the possibility that such questions might reflect unresolved issues, including the need for reconciliation and forgiveness.

Just as the psalmist called out to God in times of distress (e.g., Pss 13, 22), so today people of faith call out with similar words, seeking assurance of God's presence both now and in the life to come. Some are seeking assurance that there is in fact a life to come; they are openly dealing with their doubts and fears. Perhaps it is this area of doubt that is fertile ground for the plethora of books and websites on death, heaven, and NDEs.

Wendy Cadge, sociologist and author of *Paging God: Religion in the Halls of Medicine*, reminds us that people do call out to God from the hospital room. They are asking questions about death and afterlife. Are we listening? How are we responding? What is the basis for our response? Many are left to wonder and work out for themselves what it means to "go to heaven." What does heaven look like, smell like, and feel like? Is there a "place," or is heaven a metaphor for something else?[2]

"What does the Bible have to say?" is a question that likely is met with quite variable answers. Sadly, my experience to date is that most churchgoers don't hear much in depth from the church on this subject. I suspect that the most frequently consulted source of information is popular literature and, more recently, the Internet.

Proving Heaven

I believe it is important to read what patients and my co-workers are reading, particularly the nurses who often function as chaplains. As I read and discussed Eben Alexander's book, I was initially surprised how well it was received by those who self-reported as regular attenders in evangelical, mainline, and Catholic churches. Dr. Alexander focuses on a NDE that was obviously a life-changing experience. It is apparent the experience was quite real and meaningful to him, one to be heard with great respect. I suspect it is just this quality that draws so many to the book. Near-death experiences may be, for some, a type of epiphany, as God seeks to become known through symbols that are specific to a given culture. Carol Zaleski asks whether God, who has descended into the human condition, also descends into our cultural forms to reveal himself/herself, thereby giving us hope.[3]

When Dr. Alexander says "proof of heaven," I trust he intends to be poetic, as he expounds no universal truth or theological truth, let alone "proof." His written personal experience is proof that he did retain brain function. The fact that he is still with us and he is speaking of the experience is proof that he never really left us. Dr. Alexander makes the bold claim that he had engaged with some form of consciousness that was in no way limited by his brain.[4] No matter how depressed his cerebral function, he was there, and so was his brain (thank God and great medical care!). Dr. Alexander offers proof only that he has had a very meaningful and life-changing experience. In poetic terms his experience arises from his heart more than his brain. He neither addresses significant theological or biblical questions nor asks others to do so. He ignores a large body of literature that goes back centuries. He seems to be unaware of Carol Zaleski's works. What stands out in her work are the common threads in NDEs over the centuries.

Readers of Alexander's book need to be aware that there are many recorded NDEs. In a 1981 Gallup survey, fifteen percent of Americans reported a "close brush" with death. Thirty-four percent of these described a NDE. They are almost universally transformative. They have been discussed in theological and spiritual literature for centuries. Some describe an "out-of-body experience," a sense of having gone on a journey and/or seeing their lives pass in front of them. A prominent light may be seen; a strong or overwhelming sense of warmth and love may be experienced. The key word here is *experience*. They are not objective and not meant to be the subject of a scientific probe. And they are certainly not "proof of heaven," but, again, they are often very meaningful and life-changing experiences. I tend to hear them with respect and wonder, but never with a sense of "he/she made that up."

In medicine I have found the more that is written about a subject, the less we actually know with any degree of certainty. The prolific writing reflects our search for answers that do not now exist and possibly never will be discovered. We often write of our impressions, our speculations, or our proposed courses of action. The perceived validity of a given answer may not last past the publication date. Likewise, speculation about afterlife and heaven may bring forth a wealth of print but rarely produce answers that will meet either the demands of the heart or of human reason. I believe it is our faith that is seeking understanding, an understanding not likely found on the top shelf at Barnes & Noble or on the *New York Times* bestseller list.

Much has been written about heaven in popular literature but little agreed upon. We may be paying more attention to what popular culture has to say than does Scripture, which is, in fact, comparatively little. In recent years there have been several remarkable books on death, dying, and afterlife that might be helpful to pastors, chaplains, teachers, and laypersons.[5]

Again, we in the church and in the halls of medicine cannot be dismissive of questions surrounding death and afterlife. As one pastor with a shrug of the shoulders said, "These are simply matters of the heart that people have to work out. I don't believe there are any answers." It may be more correct to say there are no answers that will bring universal agreement, but even then, we cannot dismiss them. Faith questions have their own uncertainties. Faith and doubt often coexist in a dynamic tension, raising questions at one time or the other about our basic beliefs, including death and afterlife. At no other time do the questions and uncertainties become so important as they do when critical illness or impending death come into play.

Our hope in the resurrection and life after death is based on faith, not on reason. Reason makes us aware of the reality of death but does not carry us beyond. I have yet to attend or officiate a funeral that did not at least mention afterlife and, in many cases, raise questions. It is likely that we will keep asking the questions, as reason may not be able to understand what our faith claims. But would it not behoove the church to take the time to look at what Scripture has to say and to ask the questions that confront us as we face death?

Shortly after I shared the above thoughts, Dr. Cynthia Campbell, past president of McCormick Theological Seminary and now pastor of Highland Presbyterian Church in Louisville, delivered a sermon, "Revelation: A Glimpse of Heaven." Dr. Campbell noted that as John gets to the end of his visions, he sees a new heaven and new earth. She said, "This is the first thing to say about heaven: it is not an end but a radically new beginning! At the end of things, God starts over.... This is the first idea about heaven: the end is in fact a new beginning in which our most important relationship is restored." She continued, "Whatever heaven is, it is not for us as isolated individuals. It is for US—for the human family as a whole living in peace and harmony as the Creator envisioned."[6] Yes, there it is again—community! Even heaven is about community, about being together and relating in harmony and, yes, perhaps, recognizing the other.

More than a few colleagues have told me that they simply do not hear questions about death from their patients and only a few from families. Charles Taylor, the author of *The Secular Age*, one of the most important works of our time, offers the notion that we don't know how to deal with death; therefore, with discussions of afterlife or heaven, we avoid the subject for as long as possible.[7] Those who are dying may be eager to talk about death and what it means, but we as physicians and chaplains, projecting our own reluctance to deal with it, are prone to not pick up on this desire. Instead, we focus on offering yet another possible cure, thereby avoiding death and the difficult discussions that attend it.

There is an understandable strong desire on the part of some families to not let go of the one who is at the end of life even when it is clear that further treatment is futile. There is, therefore, little desire to talk about what death means and what might come after death. Once death comes, the question "Will I see him again?" becomes more important and often reflects unfinished business and the grounds for extended grief and guilt feelings. All considered, should we not offer more opportunities in our churches to talk about death and afterlife? As I pose such questions to pastors, seminary professors, and even some chaplains, I am often met by silence. Our views may vary significantly; however, even if we cannot all agree, don't we still owe our congregants our best? Do we wait until they are on their deathbeds, woefully ill in the hospital and crying out to God? Do we leave dealing with such questions to the family, hospital staff, and chaplains, who may not be equipped or may not share the views of the patient's particular tradition? Do we abdicate the task to the "top shelf" popular religious books at Barnes & Noble? For heaven's sake, let us hope not!

Doubt, Uncertainty, and Faith Seeking Understanding

I have wandered around a bit with this discussion prompted by "Will I see him again?" The reader is now justified to ask, "Well, Bill, what is your answer to the question?" If you are expecting me to answer with absolute certainty, you might be disappointed. A measured uncertainty has been my constant companion most of my professional life. As a child neurologist I saw infants who had sustained brain insults with resultant abnormal brain imaging studies. Invariably, I was asked to render a prognosis: What would this child look like neurologically in a few years? Would he be able to walk or run or throw a ball? Or would he be confined to a wheelchair or to the bed? I felt I was always on shaky ground if and when I prognosticated. Experience had taught me I could never say anything with certainty, at least with the degree of certainty (and therefore reassurance) parents who have gone through weeks or month of keeping vigil in the neonatal or pediatric ICU would desire. How often have I seen brain imaging studies showing missing areas of the brain, strokes, atrophy, and malformations that prompted me to think the child probably would not walk. Then, perhaps months or years later, here she would come bouncing into my clinic with only a little tightness in her heel cords or hamstrings. How often have I been concerned a child might not be able to talk or understand only to find myself, months later, carrying on a conversation with that same child.

I trained in neurology during a time of dramatic transition in our diagnostic capabilities through technology, a source of a lot of our medical certainty. Computerized tomography was quite slow in the late 1970s. What we do today in a few minutes took up to two hours. The images were not that clear. MRI was in its infancy and available in only a few centers. We relied on procedures that had some risks to them and could also cause prolonged discomfort such as headaches. To visualize the brain's anatomy we did cerebral angiography, which involves injecting contrast material into the arteries of the brain. As a neurologist-in-training I came to know every named blood vessel in the brain as I did studies in the middle of the night with the neuroradiologist at my side. I did an occasional pneumoencephalogram. The patient sat straddling a chair with his back to me. I then removed cerebrospinal fluid by way of a spinal tap, followed by injecting air, which would rise to the brain. The air would appear as a black area or void on plain skull x-rays, outlining the ventricles or chambers of fluid in the brain. As a result of the study, the patient almost always had several days of terrific headaches.

Because our studies in the late 1970s carried such morbidity or ill side effects, we did them only if necessary. We relied on a diagnostic tool that slowly fell into disuse with advancing technology: clinical judgment based on a detailed medical history and physical exam focused on the nervous system. Even at their best my clinical judgment and the available diagnostic tools left me with some degree of lingering uncertainty with every patient I saw. "Certainty" was not a part of my vocabulary then; however, I went on, stilled by the knowledge that I was doing my best as I continuously reevaluated my conclusions to the benefit of my patients.

Even as uncertainty was and is ever-present in the practice of medicine, a dynamic tension between certainty and uncertainty came early in my spiritual development. In my teens I was a member of a group of Christian young people that met in our high school after hours, the Good News Club. The group was something like Youth for Christ, a fairly conservative evangelical group. Our citywide leader was a tireless Baptist minister, Chip Miller. Every Sunday night Chip would have us gather after evening worship, a mainstay of Baptists at that time. Dozens of young people would gather at whatever church the pastor would welcome us and have what we called a "Sing-spiration." I recall the fragments of one song that asked if you had any doubts about being "born again." Later, there is a reference to having no doubts as we face eternity, a clear reference to heaven. As young conservative evangelicals the fate of our souls after death was the ultimate focus of our church life. Being "saved," hence on a track to heaven, was priority number one. Even our humor reflected this concern as we joked about having our "pie in the sky by and by." From those who were quite convinced, there came an inevitable air of certainty, sometimes of arrogant certainty, that made me more aware of my own uncertainty. This uncertainty, this doubt, has continued to this day, but not as an unwelcomed guest. My faith would not be seeking understanding if I knew all things with certainty, if I had no doubts.

The very question "Will I see him again in heaven?" in a sense betrays our own condition, for there would be no reason to ask the question if we had no uncertainties or doubts. So when I sit at the bedside and hear questions about heaven, I am comfortable and at ease, for such are my own questions as well. I suspect such questions will linger until my death. As I read scripture having to do with salvation, heaven, and resurrection, I find wiggle room. When I was much younger and certain about all faith matters, questions about heaven had crystal-clear answers. But most of those answers were based on either a literalist reading of Scripture or a theology that had no basis in Scripture at all. Many of the ideas we have about heaven are culturally derived. Such ideas become quite attractive to those looking for reassurance.

Knowing that what I have to say here will not sit well with some, I must confess that both the Gospels and Paul's letters leave me with uncertainties and questions about exactly what will happen when and how it will look. I do not find such mysteries to be problematic, for they are occasions for faith to do its work. If I knew the answers with certainty, how would that be faith?

Overall, I can find assurance that we will somehow be in the presence of the Lord; understanding will come by and by. I trust in the truth of Paul's words: "For now we see in a mirror dimly, but then we will see face to face. Now I know only in part; then I will know fully, even as I have been fully known." (1 Cor 13:12)

Yes, certainty is not necessarily ours to claim; questions abound, even "Will I see him again in heaven?"

Heaven Must Be Nearby

I took my pager and found a seat
next to a lady more pale than I.

A pink turban hid what all knew;
her sallow features said the rest.

Awkward silence—who would speak first?
My pager vibrated; I stood to go.

Her eyes, soft blue;
her smile—words fail.

I nodded and turned away
to surrender more blood.

I looked back to see
once more this phoenix.

She was no longer…but where?
Had she taken flight?

Angels do things like that.
Heaven must be nearby.

Bill Holmes
Oncology Clinic
November 2016

Notes

[1]Eben Alexander, *Proof of Heaven: A Neurosurgeon's Journey into the Afterlife* (New York: Simon & Schuster, 2012).

[2]Wendy Cadge, *Paging God: Religion in the Halls of Medicine* (Chicago: University of Chicago Press, 2013), 13.

[3]Carol Zaleski, *Life in the World to Come: Near-Death Experience and Christian Hope* (Oxford: Oxford University Press, 1996), 24.

[4]Alexander, *Proof of Heaven*, 9.

[5]Recommended books on dying, death, and afterlife: Fred Craddock, Dale Goldsmith, and Joy Goldsmith, *Speaking of Dying: Recovering the Church's Voice in the Face of Death* (Grand Rapids: Brazos Press, 2012); Allen Verhey, *The Christian Art of Dying* (Grand Rapids: Eerdmans, 2013); Rob Moll, *The Art of Dying: Living Fully into the Life to Come* (Downer's Grove: InterVarsity Press, 2010); Susan Garrett, *No Ordinary Angel: Celestial Spirits and Christian Claims about Jesus* (New Haven: Yale University Press, 2008). Professor Garrett offers an in-depth discussion of death and afterlife. Garrett notes that Old Testament images of heaven may offer us a picture of a divine council room or royal court, or a temple, with the inhabitants being primarily engaged in giving honor to God. She goes on to remind us that many will be dismayed to learn that Jesus, the Gospels, and Paul have little to say about what happens between death and the general resurrection.

[6]Cynthia Campbell, "Revelation: A Glimpse of Heaven," sermon preached at Highland Presbyterian Church, April 28, 2013. Used with permission.

[7]Charles Taylor, *The Secular Age* (Cambridge: The Belknap Press of Harvard University, 2007), 25–26.

CHAPTER 6

A Journey to Hope

When I started this essay, I found myself staring at the computer screen for extended periods of time. I struggled to find a starting place; I am still struggling. What does it mean to hope? Is hope something we just have or something we experience?

There are a few things that hope is not. Hope is not wishful thinking, a desire for this or that, or just optimism. Hope is not simply a view of last things or end times. Raise hope questions in a room full of folks who have long been in church and attention will turn to eschatology followed by a brief period of communal questioning of your faith if you don't adhere to what they already hold to be true. But I am getting far ahead of myself. Please be patient with me as I relate my journey to near-hopelessness and the subsequent journey back to hope.

In summer 1980 I completed my training in neurology with an emphasis on child neurology. Joyce and I packed up our stuff, buckled our two daughters in the back seat of our Pontiac, and drove to Louisville with the family dog, a chocolate poodle named Brandy, sitting in Joyce's lap as though she was riding "shotgun." Brandy was, in fact, in charge of the car.

A few days later, on July 1, in an act that set the tone for the next decade, I started practicing neurology while my wife and daughters joined two of our best friends and their daughters for a beach vacation. I joined two bright adult neurologists in an extremely busy practice that covered neurological consultations in three downtown Louisville hospitals serving primarily adults. One of my new associates had also been standing in the gap and seeing children for several years, as no one was doing full-time child neurology in Louisville. Over the next thirteen years I saw children primarily but also helped with the high volume of adult consultations. This arrangement translated into very long workdays. Most days I was in the hospital parking lot by 6:30 a.m., if not earlier. Most evenings I did not get home until 10 p.m. The exception was Tuesday, because

I was officially listed as having Tuesday afternoon off. That usually meant I saw children in the office who could not wait for the next available routine appointment. These were usually children with the recent onset of seizures, intractable headaches, or tic disorders such as Tourette syndrome. Getting home at 6 p.m. on Tuesday was a real relief. On other weekdays there were always those who had to be seen sooner rather than later. Since the office staff needed to go home at some reasonable time, I would see the children in the orthopedic cast room of the Kosair Children's Hospital ER between 6 and 8 p.m.

Before long my short weeks were roughly sixty hours. My long weeks, those on which I was the weekend call doctor, were about eighty hours. The next decade looked pretty much like this without letting up. I would take a week off in the summer to go to the beach with my family. Even there, I found myself talking to parents by phone and giving instructions for changing or manipulating medication to control seizures or headaches. In a sense I was never really gone from the practice; I had only changed my location and mode of care. I had become a "workaholic."[1]

Needless to say, there is a price to be paid for "workaholism." Rather than consuming alcohol to the point of adversely affecting my health and relationships, I worked and worked and worked and then worked some more. I had a hard time ever refusing to see a patient in timely fashion, even when the request was probably not reasonable. It was as though I was driven by a sense of "ought."

By the late 1980s I was on the road to burnout. I recall the intense feeling of hopelessness. I did not look for a way out. After all, I was doing what I felt "called" to do, just as a preacher feels called to preach. But such a sense of higher calling does not exempt anyone from paying the price for failing to do self-care. Even though I saw myself as doing what I had been called by God to do, there was little joy. Along with hopelessness came a certain resignation that declared, "This is how things are, so live in this moment." At first glance that might pass as good advice, but such advice left me feeling empty more often than not. If what I saw of my life, using the lens of my innermost self, was the fullness of what I had worked for, anticipated, and, in hope, at one time prayed for, then despair was about to become my constant companion. Although people surrounded me, I felt alone and lonely. I had no sense of community.

At the time I tended to define my religious and spiritual self more in terms of being a deacon, Sunday school teacher, church committee member—all the outward signs of religiosity and piety. There clearly was little or no spiritual depth. I could talk the "Jesus talk" with the best of them. Eventually, even Sunday worship had either been put aside altogether or relegated to a mostly perfunctory activity. Times of prayer and reflection were essentially nonexistent. At the same time I was working eighty-hour weeks with rarely a day off. I lacked real perspective on what I was doing. The practice of medicine began to lose meaning for me. My sense of ministry slowly eroded and withered away. I was engulfed by a sense of hopelessness.

I have a history of intellectualizing the stressors I meet in life. Being one who likes to read, I started wading through the shelves of Hawley-Cooke Bookstore. I "hoped" to find something to read about hope, as I was finding that I knew little about it personally. After a few hours of browsing, I happened upon Jürgen Moltmann's *Theology of Hope*.[2] Anyone who has engaged Moltmann at all knows that his works do not lend themselves to understanding by a rank amateur, especially a cynical child neurologist tottering on the edge of burnout. I read the first ninety-four pages and stopped. I know that because my margin notes cease at that point. I am a compulsive margin-scribbler and underliner.

Moltmann seems to say that we find ourselves just accepting the present, no matter what it is like, as the way things must be, so live on! On the other hand we might expect things to get better one day and look forward to that day so much that we fail to live in today. The result is unhappiness.[3] I was always thinking of what I had to do next, what I MUST do next, and in doing so my present moment was never fully my focus.

I agree with Moltmann that we come to know God as God acts on our lives. Note that is God acting upon us; God is taking the initiative. Certainly we can and do pray, meditate, study Scripture, and worship with the desire (hope) of both knowing and being known. However, in the final analysis it is the Spirit acting on us that informs and transforms us. A problem arises when we are not available to hear the voice of God when we are too busy "doing." Such was the case with me in the late 1980s and early 1990s. My spiritual life was nonexistent. I functioned like a highly productive assembly-line worker or an automaton. Burnout was becoming quite apparent by the late 1980s.

The Kingdom Within

At the urging of a friend, I sought counseling from a pastoral care center in a local church. The counselor assigned to me was Dr. Leigh Conver, now a personal friend. About the same time I was reading and rereading John A. Sanford's *The Kingdom Within: The Inner Meaning of Jesus' Sayings*. I could spend a long time sharing the multiple underlined and re-marked passages. Suffice it to say for now that I began standing outside Elijah's cave and listening for the voice of God, but I heard only silence. It was not because God was not speaking, but because either I did not know how to listen or I did not speak God's language. Sanford made me aware of God's forgotten language—dreams. With the encouragement of my therapist, who was trained in pastoral care and counseling by Dr. Wayne E. Oates, I began to record any and all dreams. At first I had no dreams I could remember. Then, the first thing each morning, I started recording the fragments I could recall. Then came the one dream that engaged me at the deepest level; it was what some have called a "numinous" dream, a dream that is clearly a spiritual experience leaving one full of awe and wonder. The dream's effect has been long lasting. I still recall the feeling of the hair on the back of my neck standing up as well as the trembling of my hands. I share this dream in hopes that others will at least consider the possibility that God speaks through dreams. In this particular instance I think such was the case. Here are the exact words recorded in my journal:

> Dream on 6-9-92, awakening at 4 a.m.
>
> The most detailed and one of the most vivid dreams I have ever had. I woke up excited, grabbed a cup of coffee, and started writing:
>
> I am invited to go on a boat. It looks like a barge, but it is like a sub. It is old. We enter from the end. There are many men and a few women. They identify themselves as scientist, biologist, and old sub sailors. One of the women (dressed in sheer pale green dress) and one man start pulling big levers up and down to power the generators. We are told that we should each take our turn to keep the sub moving. As we do so, I see a great wave of water coming from the front and get a little unnerved. The lady in green explains that we have opened the front door to let water in so we can submerge. The force of the water seems to be about to push the inner walls of the boat down. Some of

the walls are Plexiglas whose screws and bolts are broken, perhaps from age—the boat looks old.

I call for the captain and set to helping him repair the bolt. I placed a long screw in the fiberglass and into the steel support—surprisingly, it holds—despite the crack in the Plexiglas—the captain compliments me.

The crew gets together at mid-ship—sitting around bunks and under blankets. It is chilly [off in the margin of the narrative, I wrote, "My fat abdomen at one point is sticking out, and I cover it with my sweatshirt—I am embarrassed"). Suddenly, the boat is rocking and jerking. I inquire as to why the trip is so rough. We are under the sea—I thought it would be smoother...I am told we are going over under-sea mountains. The sea is under the earth, and we are on our way to Denver—I say, "Great, I have never been there."

The boat suddenly is emerging from the water and running along the ground, making a groove as we go. We are knocking down fences as we go. I feel uncomfortable that we are damaging property, but the captain tells me he has received prior permission for this route.

We stop on the edge of little rural town. The boat's crew opens the end of the boat. It looks like they are going to sell things like at a roadside stand.

I get off the boat and start walking down the street. There are some old shops and a small gas station. Across the street is a theatre-like building with a sign saying, "Tillie—for all ages." At first I don't go in because it is probably a "peep show" but the temptation wins out and I go in. There are young people standing around talking. Some are smoking. The room to the right is filled with old musical instruments, the other room with unidentifiable objects. I start back out, and off to right is a smoking room. I entered. To the left are men standing in suits and overcoats, laughing and looking into booths. There is a ticket taker at the door. I recall thinking, "No, this isn't for me." I leave, and as I go, a man who looks familiar to me starts to walk with me. He is muttering about how disquieting the place is. As I leave, I note my boat is gone. I get slightly frantic but note a dirt path torn up by the boat as it crossed the road and up the hill. I started running along the path toward the boat. As I ran up the hill, the crew stood on the boat and gave me a lighthearted salute and welcome. I awaken—I have never been so excited about a dream. I have been nearly in tears of joy as I write.

I interpret the dream as meaning I am going on a journey—an inward journey that many others have made (old sailors). It will be rough. I will have to work and be creative, but there is a captain that will be in charge and help me make the repairs. I will have to supply some but not all of the power. It will get rough due to the inward mountains. I will get off the boat and be tempted to take wrong pathways, but I will be welcomed back to the boat (forgiven?).

At the time I did not see the woman in green as being part of me. It was years later before I asked myself about the identity of the familiar-looking person who walked out of Tillie's with me. What part of me was he? Or was this a reconnection to the spiritual part of me? [end of journal record]

I saw this dream as marking the beginning of a spiritual journey that is still ongoing. I began to be more aware of God as revealed in Jesus Christ. I had not yet been introduced to the idea of the "already but not yet" with respect to the kingdom of God, that kingdom I had prayed for numerous times as I prayed the Lord's Prayer. I began to understand the kingdom of God as a present reality, the "already." Sanford made me aware of the kingdom of God as a reality to be lived in, not just talked about.[4] My conservative evangelical background had made me much more aware of the transcendent nature of the kingdom and, with that, the question of exactly what comes after this earthly existence. After all, wasn't it all about going to heaven and escaping hell?

There ensued an ineffective spiritual search for meaning in the "now," a search that was hardly enough to change how I was living my life. I would need to journey into the wilderness for change to happen. I continued working long hours in a burnt out state for another year. My goal appeared to be "Save the Pediatric Neurologist," rather than changing the way I lived my life. On March 8, 1993, I got home from the hospital at 2 a.m. Sitting on the deck overlooking the remains of winter's brown hues mixed with the early spring budding of a large maple, I knew that I could not go on or I would soon be dead. I was already spiritually and emotionally on "life support." The battle to save the pediatric neurologist had been lost! I gave my office and the University of Louisville six months' notice after sunrise that very day. I left practice and teaching August 31, 1993, and headed into the wilderness. That which I loved doing had consumed me. It would take a year to make my way back from the wilderness and return to medical practice.

The Wilderness

The wilderness is a strange place. It is that place where my soul waits in silence for God, the source of my hope (see Ps 62:1–5). Yes, the wild things are there, but there also is the silence of waiting. The external demands cease as I find space for just being. Waiting patiently in the wilderness has to be one of the most difficult tasks ever. Surely, I reasoned, I have to be doing something. Why is my beeper not going off? I no longer had a beeper hanging on my belt to bail me out. I would have to learn to wait quietly and patiently as I sat in the wilderness. I scribbled many pages of notes in my journal during that first three months.

On September 1, 1993, I wrote that I gave up everything to survive as a pediatric neurologist. I had quit teaching Sunday school, resigned from the deacon board, given up golf or anything else that resembled play, made no new friends, and abandoned many of my old ones. Most of my relationships had been patient-doctor, as husband-wife, father–daughter, brother-sibling, and friend-friend had all been either neglected or not well nourished. At the time I felt that the only way I could begin to recover was to step away from the very thing that had consumed me, the practice of pediatric neurology. But move away to what? I had no clue.

The first few weeks were marked by multiple calls from the parents of longtime patients. They were upset with me on the one hand but understood on the other. They asked what they were to do now for medical care for their seriously impaired children. At the time I was reading Henri Nouwen's *In the Name of Jesus*. He points out that Jesus' first temptation was to be relevant by turning the stone into bread. Bread is good, for it sustains us as well as feeds the hungry. Spending every hour of every day caring for neurologically impaired kids, as good a thing as that is, had become my point of relevancy. In the practice of pediatric neurology, I had earned a reputation of always being there, day and night, like a "super doc." And while I was seeking to be relevant, the price I paid was lack of sleep, lack of quality personal time, and lack of meaningful relationships with my wife, family, and friends. I was too busy being relevant as a physician, which, like turning stone into bread, looks good and even feels good, but then things get out of balance. Now that balance needed to be restored.

Protest, depression, and apathy are three levels of lostness of a neglected and lonely soul.[5] In my humanness I was now learning to struggle with fear and face aloneness. I refer here to what I felt inwardly, for there were people all around me. The danger I faced was settling for easy answers about my fears and sense of loneliness instead of wrestling with what it means to be in a divine-human relationship. I had forgotten about God. Questions of faith and hope began to take center stage and have yet to exit.

The Faith to Hope

The apparent contradictions between God's promises and the extremes of suffering can and do challenge faith and question hope. It is not surprising to hear these words in the halls of medicine: "If there is a loving God, how can this happen?" In the midst of the harsh reality of suffering, are the promises of God really pointing to some future time, thereby giving us "guaranteed" hope? At least, that is what I heard often in the church of my youth and beyond. The rejoinder to my questioning has most often been, "Our hope for the future is *certain*, for it is based on the crucifixion and resurrection of Jesus Christ." But if we know for certain, if our hope for the future is guaranteed, then is it still hope? Did not Paul the apostle say, "For in hope we are saved. Now hope that is seen is not hope. For who hopes for what is seen?" (Rom 8:24)?

So what is the ultimate source of our hope as Christians? Is it not a hope that arises from our faith in God as revealed in the story of Jesus Christ who lived, died a horrible death, and was resurrected from the dead? The very foundation of Christianity has been this narrative. Without such hope in the crucified and resurrected Jesus, faith starts to disintegrate.[6]

The hope that comes to us through faith in the resurrected Jesus somehow affects our present as well as our future. Living in the present hope means seeing the reality of the "now" and learning to live in it while looking to a future reality. Moltmann argued that faith without such hope risks becoming something other than Christian faith, and hope without faith in the living God risks becoming nothing more than optimism.[7]

When we speak of hope in the context of an illness, are we thinking of "clinical hope," hope based on what medicine may do for us? After all, we are about to trust the world of medicine to save us from the rapidly multiplying cells that we call "cancer." As Christians we certainly hope that modern medicine can cure our cancer, palliate our pain, and give us more meaningful days. Nonetheless, do we not somehow inexplicably find our ultimate hope in God's mysterious gift, Jesus Christ?

Hope should never be confused with some strong feeling that everything is going to turn out well (i.e., optimism). Hope in Jesus Christ is not, in human terms, "outcome dependent." Do not think I am discounting clinical hope, for it is often the driving force that prompts some, if not many, to continue with treatment such as chemotherapy. In end-of-life stories hope might be found in the simple expectation that something good can come in the midst of suffering, even the suffering associated with the side effects of chemotherapy and radiation. The hope for a remission or miracle cure might well occupy the thoughts of many as they face the end of life. Perhaps such makes life as it is more tolerable. Who can be critical of that?

When faced with a critical or debilitating illness, a cancer pronouncement, or the beginning of chemotherapy with its varied side effects, periods of all-consuming grief might overtake us. In our mourning we raise our protest, our complaint, our lament to God. It is there that we ask questions and raise our doubts. But in that same moment there is hope that lingers at the back of our minds, stepping forward from time to time, then receding into the shadows once again as we see the reality of our predicament.

Some might say, "Do not mourn, but have faith and hope." But the Beatitudes say, "Blessed are those who mourn" (Matt 5:4). So is not mourning itself a Christian practice?[8]

Lament and hope can and do travel together. To lament without hope is to open ourselves to ongoing despair. To hope without lament is naïve optimism. To neither hope nor lament is to be stoically detached from reality, denying that anything has happened. "Faithful suffering" entails both lament and hope as we face the reality of our own finitude or the loss of a loved one.[9]

Elsewhere in this book, I share some thoughts on community. Suffice it to say here that our sense of hope can be diminished due to a lack of community. In our society there is a great emphasis on individualism. Even in the church we hear much about "my personal relationship to Jesus" but relatively little about community-building as part of our faith journey. Surely we are to live out our faith in a community of the faithful where we can come to a sense of meaning and an understanding of our own vulnerable condition. Recall that Jesus surrounded himself with others, first the Twelve, then all who would come. He repeatedly called them to gather around the table to share a meal, for it is there, in the intimate face-to-face time of sharing stories around the table, that both the spirit and the body are nourished and intimacy is nurtured. We are prone to see faith as just between the individual and God, so we fail to build community. I am encouraged when the suffering one asks for prayer for those he will leave behind while making no specific requests for himself. What is important at death is the community that has given meaning to our lives. Should not that same community be the intentional focus of our lives? In the midst of our work, no matter how important it may seem to be, it is building and maintaining of community that offers hope.

Ultimately, I believe hope is relational in its origins, birthed and nourished by the Holy Spirit as we learn to live and love in community with others. It is there I find hope.

Notes

[1]Wayne E. Oates, *Confessions of a Workaholic: The Facts about Work Addiction* (Waco: Word Publishing Co., 1972).

[2]Jürgen Moltmann, *Theology of Hope: On the Ground and the Implications of a Christian Eschatology* (Minneapolis: Fortress Press, 1993), 26.

[3]Ibid., 52.

[4]John A. Sanford, *The Kingdom Within: The Inner Meaning of Jesus' Sayings*, rev. ed. (San Francisco: Harper & Row, 1987), 41.

[5]Henri Nouwen, *The Road to Daybreak: A Spiritual Journey* (New York: Image, 1990), 77.

[6]Moltmann, *Theology of Hope*, 34.

[7]Ibid., 37.

[8]Kelly M. Kapic, *Embodied Hope: A Theological Meditation on Pain and Suffering* (Downer's Grove: IVP Academic, 2017), 30.

[9]Ibid., 31.

CHAPTER 7

Psalms on the Ground

Life is a psalm; it begins with crying out mixed with the joy of being and ends with thanksgiving. The in-between is a journey marked by giving and receiving, doing good and not-so-good, faith and doubt, rethinking and rebirth, repentance and grace, hope, and love.

Bill Holmes
"Scribblings"
May 2013

Some psalms seem to have been written by those well acquainted with suffering, people not unlike those I encounter daily in the hospital now journeying in a wilderness of disorientation. Hearing the news that something bad is happening or about to happen, that failing organs or rapidly dividing cells threaten their very lives, the suffering one cries out to God. For some it may be the first words they have ever uttered to God, but for many others who have been on a life-long journey of faith, invoking the presence of the divine is part of who they are. The psalms of lament (e.g., 10, 13, 22, 42, 77) speak to such times.

The lament psalms and all that might be said about them have become quite meaningful and real in my own life. As I have faced life-threatening illnesses, I have turned again and again to the psalms, for they speak to what is deep within my very being. In addition to mitral valve heart surgery, on four different occasions I have heard, "Bill, you have cancer" (see ch. 3 for more about my own journeys with cancer). The sense of being alone and facing the terrible unknown prompted me to cry out to God in protest, not just as protest and complaint but also as a visceral prayer, a gut-level response to what was happening. There was an admixture of anger, complaint, wondering why, and feeling alone as one standing in the middle of the desert with nothing in sight but sand, rugged terrain, and wild things. The vastness of what my inner vision conjured up was at first overwhelming.

The lament is a prayer to God as a response to trouble. Those crying out might neither mention God by name nor readily identify as persons of faith, but I suspect that whatever idea they do have of the divine somehow comes into play. Their prayers of lament reveal their faith and trust in a God they may not know well, but they know well enough.

As I have read the psalms with those who are facing the unspeakable and pondering questions they have never before asked, I have seen smiles of recognition, heard gasps of surprise, and witnessed tears of hope.

It is with the psalms in my heart that I am called to the bedside to lean in to another's wilderness. The wilderness can be a place of renewal, of getting away from the grind to reflect and pray. Jesus went into the wilderness to rest, pray, and even teach. To go to such a wilderness is often a choice we make to recuperate and reflect. But there are other wildernesses to which we do not choose to journey but, as humans, we all face eventually. They are dangerous and disorienting places, places we would rather avoid. Most often we are not given a choice about such journeys; we are simply compelled from within to go.

I am often called to be with one who has been thrust into the unimaginable. I approach the edge of that person's wilderness to listen. I say "the edge" because I believe I can never fully appreciate what is going on inwardly for the one who has just learned that death may not be far away. Sometimes I hear only silence. At other times I hear cries coming from deep within her wilderness. I remain silent, listening without commenting, unless requested verbally or nonverbally. The crying out of another's heart in a time of disorientation or disordering of life can best be heard when we are silent. Otherwise, we risk becoming background noise that keeps the other from being heard or from hearing God. At such times God seems to speak in a whisper or not at all.

Encounters in the wilderness are largely with our own ideas and thoughts. However, the wilderness traveler also encounters others who are prone to speak but not listen. They either tell the traveler there is no way out or there is a way if you do this or that. Often it is the visitor trying to reassure himself as the specter of a fellow traveler facing the unspeakable prompts anxiety and dread, so much so that he is made acutely aware of his own fragile human state. At times the voices may be from those who want to "fix" everything and still others who would chide the suffering one for the lack of faith that got him into the wilderness in the first place. Perhaps there should be a sign on every hospital room door that reads, "Fixers need not enter." The one journeying in the wilderness does not need to be fixed so much as she needs to be heard. So often at the bedside the discomfort of the visitor prompts so much verbiage that the cries from the wilderness of the suffering one are drowned out.

When I go to the edge of another's wilderness, there are three things I do: clear the clutter, lean in, and listen. I do so because others have done so for me and, in doing so, have become my teachers. In May 2016 I experienced chest discomfort as I walked quickly through the ICU to be with a family whose father had just died. I stopped briefly to lean on the desk in the nurses' station. The pain cleared, and I continued on my way to be with the bereaved family. As I left the ICU, I told another the chaplain what had happened. He urged me to go to the ER. I had no plans to spend the rest of the day on a gurney. Besides, I had just had a stress test nine months ago. I did call my internal medicine doctor, who had me come to his office that afternoon to have an ECG. Although my ECG was unchanged from nine months ago, he set up a gadolinium stress test for the next morning.

During the stress test I again had chest discomfort without ECG changes per my reading. The staff doing the tests knew I could read EEGs but did not ask if I could read ECGs as well. It is not that I do it well, but I know enough.

I left the lab feeling fine, but a few hours later I received a call from my doctor telling me I had failed the stress test. I suppose I had not studied hard enough for the test. I was told to see my cardiologist the next morning. Upon arrival in his office, I received a brief lecture on why I should have gone to the ER when I had the chest pain. My stupidity not withstanding, I was scheduled for cardiac angiography in two days.

I arrived in the cardiac catheterization lab looking calm on the outside, but I was apprehensive on the inside. I was no stranger to invasive cardiac studies. Fourteen years earlier my cardiologist discovered a murmur when I was having a checkup for a controlled cardiac arrhythmia. I recall vividly the look on his face as he listened to my heart for more than the usual amount of time. He then asked, "Bill, have you listened to your heart lately?" Some doctors do things like that; I was not one of them then, but I am now. My reply was quick and quippy: "Have you done an EEG on yourself lately?" I will not relate all he said then, but it put me in the right frame of mind to hear, "You have a problem. Your mitral valve has a major leak."

Several more tests and five weeks later I was in the open-heart surgery suite at Jewish Hospital having my chest cracked open. Yes, the neurologist who had come to the post-op recovery area more times than he could remember to evaluate the neurologic status of a heart surgery patient was now about to go on the heart-lung bypass machine. The doctor who had seen post-op patients with altered mental statuses, weak or flaccid limbs, blindness in one eye or both, peripheral nerve compressions, and the worst deficit of all—failure to wake up from surgery—was about to take his turn.

I had been given a list of possible complications (as if I did not know them already). I must have checked all of them except death. I had been told I would not be intubated when I woke up; however, I was. My hands were restrained so I, in my foggy state, would not pull the endotracheal tube out. Eventually, the tube was removed, and I began to wake up more. As a physician I was trained to observe and listen, so there in the middle of the night in the open-heart recovery unit, I did just that. I noticed my skin was sallow. Why? My hemoglobin was 7.0, not a normal 12–14. Then, like any decent neurologist, I did a brief neurological exam on myself. My right hand and wrist were weak and numb. I informed my nurse, who promptly said, "Yes, and you are going for a CT scan of your brain as soon as we think you are stable enough." The CT was normal; the weakness was secondary to peripheral nerve compressions likely due to a tight blood-pressure cuff during surgery.

I was kept in a monitored bed overnight. I don't recall sleeping at all as I lay there in my uncomfortable bed listening to and watching my ECG bouncing across the multicolored displays on the monitor and weighing each and every word I heard from the several nurses in the unit. Early on post-op day two I began to experience a funny feeling in my chest, and about the same time, I heard a nurse say, "Bed number ten—atrial fibrillation." I was in bed number ten! Over the next several days I went into atrial fib-flutter and quickly into heart failure, taking on several pounds of fluid weight. I was short of breath as they moved me back to a monitored bed. My anxiety level then was exceeded only by the level I had just before surgery.

Now, fourteen years later, I again was lying in a cardiac catheterization lab. This time I was reviewing in my mind all that had happened during and after my mitral valvuloplasty, a procedure to put a space-age plastic ring around my mitral valve. Thoughts about the events surrounding summer 2002 occupied my every moment. I was in a pensive and worried state. Then came the supervisor of chaplains in the Norton Hospital system. She did not say a word at first but went about the business of making a path to the side of my gurney. She had to move a rolling table, a computer on wheels, and one of two chairs to gain access to the side of my temporary abode. She pulled up a chair, sat down, leaned in toward me, and gently asked how I was doing. She already knew how I was doing; she could read it in my face. For the next thirty minutes she simply listened to me recount how I got to this point. I threw in how this felt compared to other times I waited in the wilderness of pre-op or post-op areas at the time of heart or cancer surgery. I could feel the anxiety diminishing and a sense of reassurance and peace coming over me. By the time the nurse showed up at the door to announce that it was time to go, I was at peace with whatever. My chaplain had offered no advice. Beyond an initial greeting and a brief prayer at the end, she had said little in words. However, her leaning in and listening sent a message of comfort and caring that helped me through a wilderness wandering in the cardiac cath lab. There were no lions and tigers roaring, no rattlesnakes hissing, no dense jungle to fight my way through, no treacherous cliffs, but a wilderness nonetheless.

I was given a small dose of a benzodiazepine just before the cardiac cath. I recall hearing voices but don't recall much that was said until an unidentified voice said, "Things look good, Bill. Valves okay. I will go over the findings later. No stents. No surgery." By the time I got back to my holding room, my family was smiling, as they had already heard. The wilderness wandering was over for that day. Informed by my own experiences and the example set by Rev. Kelley Woggon, I go often to the pre-op area to see if anyone needs a visit. I move this or that table, rearrange chairs, move up close to the bedside, and lean in.

I am frequently asked to pray with patients going to surgery. Usually family members are present. The "religious preference" listed may be any Christian denomination, Jew, Muslim, Hindu, Buddhist, or none. I contact an imam, priest, rabbi, or cantor as needed or requested. I have them on "rapid dial."

I usually ask if there is something specific the person or the family members would like in the prayer. The answer may seem obvious to us, but the obvious is not always what I get. I often hear more concern from patients about their loved ones than I do about their own welfare. Some choose to pray aloud, and others defer to me (after all, isn't that what chaplains do?). I pray using their words as if they were praying aloud through me. The prayers are often "gut-level"; elegance takes a backseat.

From those in the Judeo-Christian tradition, I ask permission to share a psalm or ask if they have a scripture that has been particularly meaningful. Recognizing that theirs is a time of disorientation, metaphorically and perhaps literally, the chosen scripture may reflect their cry for help and/or anticipatory gratitude. A few years ago a fifty-year-old lady with a malignant tumor occupying her left brain spoke of her desire to awaken from surgery still able to speak. We read Psalm 13 together: "How long, O LORD? Will you forget me forever? How long will you hide your face from me? How long must I bear pain in my soul and have sorrow in my heart all day long? How long shall my enemy be exalted over me?" (vv. 1–2).

After those two verses she interrupted me and said in her already stuttering speech, "Psalm 13. Yes, that's me!"

Soon after her surgery I went to the ICU to see her for the first time post-op. Initially, she could utter only a few words; she knew what she wanted to say but could not speak in fluid language. With a smile she said, "You know!" Yes, I did know.

Scripture, especially psalms, often speaks directly to our human predicament. When we are in the midst of disorientation or disordering of our lives, we hear the familiar in a different way. It is one thing to hear, for instance, Psalm 22 in worship, but quite a different experience when we have just been told our lives are in danger.

What follows comes from my written and mental notes gathered over several years; they are not verbatim. I have added a fitting psalm or other scripture that I hope speaks to the prayer. The last one is mine from August 15, 2011, in Norton Hospital pre-op before colectomy for cancer.

Prayers from the Edge of the Wilderness

"I am thankful, God, that this thing they say is the size of a golf ball is not as big as a baseball. I don't know; I just don't know. I just pray my surgeon is on his game today."

Blessed be the LORD, for he has heard the sound of my pleadings. The LORD is my strength and my shield; in him my heart trusts; so I am helped and my heart exults, and with my songs I give thanks to him (Ps 28:6–7).

"Lord, I am afraid. Please let me wake up from this surgery. Please, Lord, let me recognize my family, and may they recognize me."

But you, O LORD, do not be far away! O my help, come quickly to my aid! Deliver my soul from the sword, my life from the power of the dog! Save me from the mouth of the lion! (Ps 22:19–21).

"God, I want to get on with this. I want this thing out. I have been in pain for way too long, Lord, way too long. I am tired, and my family is very tired." How long, O LORD? Will you forget me forever? How long will you hide your face from me?... But I trusted in your steadfast love; my heart shall rejoice in your salvation. I will sing to the LORD, because he has dealt bountifully with me (Ps 13:1, 5–6).

"God, I am not so much afraid for me. My prayer is that my children will be okay and my husband will have peace with whatever happens."

The LORD is my light and my salvation; whom shall I fear? The LORD is the stronghold of my life; of whom shall I be afraid? (Ps 27:1).

"Let me whisper lest anyone hear this. I am frightened and uncertain about what comes after death. My family would die if they knew. God, forgive me."

Be gracious to me, O LORD, for I am in distress; my eye wastes away from grief, my soul and body also. For my life is spent with sorrow. And my years with sighing; my strength fails because of my misery, and my bones waste away (Ps 31:9–10).

"I have no idea what to say to you, God. I'll just say, 'Hello.'"

But may all who seek you rejoice and be glad in you; may those who love your salvation say continually, "Great is the LORD!" As for me, I am poor and needy; but the LORD takes thought for me (Ps 40:16–17a).

"Tell me, Lord, will you be there when I am asleep and totally unaware of what is being done to me? I fear this loss of control. And please, if you are there, keep reminding the surgeon that you are watching."

Where can I go from your spirit? Or where can I flee from your presence? If I ascend to the heaven, you are there; if I make my bed in Sheol, you are there. If I take the wings of the morning and settle at the farthest limits of the sea, even there your hand shall lead me, and your right hand shall hold me fast (Ps 139:7–10).

"O God, my creator and deliverer, I have heard the roar of your silence in the midst of my fear of the unspeakable; I grow mute. O death, can you not wait?"

Remove the sandals from your feet, for the place on which you are standing is holy ground. Amen (Exod 3:5).

A Prayer for the Emergency Department

A few years ago I asked the nurses in our emergency department to write a brief prayer arising out of their daily experiences. I then added scripture that somehow spoke to that prayer. What follows now hangs in the staff lounge of the ED at Norton Brownsboro Hospital, Louisville.

"You know when I am doing chest compressions or when I am holding the hand of a frightened patient. You know when I am encountering a difficult family or when I am comforting the beloved of one now deceased."

O LORD, you have searched me and known me. You know when I sit down and when I rise up (Ps 139:1–2a).

"You know my anxiety and depression and understand the troubles I face at work and at home."

You discern my thoughts from far away (Ps 139:2b).

"Some who come through those doors are dirty; some are angry and mean; some just don't get it. Help me to love and care for them."

Truly I tell you, just as you did it to one of the least of these who are members of my family, you did it to me (Matt 25:40).

"Lord, when I see the horrible things that happen to people, I sometimes wonder if you are really there."

How long, O LORD? Will you forget me forever? How long will you hide your face from me? How long must I have pain in my soul, and have sorrow in my heart all day long? (Ps 13:1–2).

"Sometimes, Lord, this job is too much. My blood pressure is up, and my heart is pounding. O Lord, strengthen my compassion, and deliver me from burnout."

But those who wait for the LORD shall renew their strength, they shall mount up with wings like eagles, they shall run and not be weary, they shall walk and not faint (Isa 40:31).

"I pray that we might be instruments of peace. Grant us peace in our hearts, in our homes, in our work."

Peace I leave with you; my peace I give you…. Do not let your hearts be troubled and do not be afraid (John 14:27).

"O Lord, when I go into an exam room, I sense you are already there and, even in this wild and crazy ED, I am standing on holy ground."

Where can I go from your spirit? Or where can I flee from your presence? (Ps 139:7).

AMEN

Triangle Between I-65 and ramp to St. Catherine Street
(Engelhard School can be seen on other side of ramp)

Under the Ramp from I-65 to St. Catherine Street (2007)
(mattresses for sleeping; this ramp has since been replaced;
there is no longer any flat area that allows sleeping)

CHAPTER 8

Poverty: The Child of Injustice

"The evidence has been before us for decades that black people, other ethnic minorities, and some poor whites have been getting sick for and enduring horrible deaths from the filth they breathe, eat, drink, and otherwise ingest from the garbage dumps, landfills, incinerators, toxic waste sites, oil refineries, petrochemical plants, and other world-class generators of pollution that have been deliberately and relentlessly installed in the neighborhoods where they live, work, worship, and go to school."[1]

My habit for most of my medical career was to make my hospital rounds in the early morning before patients were being transported to radiology or other department, before a parent had to leave to go to work, and well before the medical charts had disappeared from the chart rack so the nurses or medical students could make their notes on what happened overnight. Most often I was the alarm clock for the family, letting them know a new day had begun. One mid-winter morning I entered the room of my two-year-old patient and found his parents, five siblings, two cousins, an aunt, and a grandmother all asleep on the window-seat bed, the rocking chair, or on the hard, bare floor. Virtually all were in somewhat soiled clothing. The odor in the room was pungent. A stack of hospital-issued blankets and towels were lying undisturbed near the door. I paused briefly, backed out of the room without disturbing anyone, and went in search of the nurse.

As the story unfolded, I learned that both parents dropped out of school at age sixteen. Neither parent could read or write. Only one child had been fully vaccinated for childhood diseases. Had my patient received the HIB vaccine to prevent bacterial meningitis, he would not be in the hospital. The family had not applied for any government assistance, not only because they were embarrassed to ask for help, but also because they could neither understand the process nor read the papers they received from a social worker.

My patient and his extended family were essentially homeless. According to a state social worker the last place they called home was a run-down, two-room building heated only by a wood stove and lighted by a single bulb hanging over a table in the middle of the largest room. There was no running water and no indoor toilet. In addition, the father was disabled by significant heart disease, which would take his life before winter's end.

This child's family needed someone to walk alongside them. They needed help navigating the system. I turned first to our nurses. Pediatric nurses wear multiple hats, so to speak, as they not only do the expected such as giving medications, monitoring the patient for any changes, and charting all that happens, but they also act as social workers, counselors, and even chaplains. Knowing the social problems of the patient and his family, gathering needed clothing, finding food in the middle of the night for hungry siblings, and listening to grieving and hurting parents were all acts of concern and love that were not in the nurses' job descriptions but are part of who they are. Many have an unstated practical theology based on Matthew 25:35–36 where Jesus says, "For I was hungry and you gave me food, I was thirsty and you gave me something to drink, I was a stranger and you welcomed me, I was naked and you gave me clothing, I was sick and you took care of me, I was in prison and you visited me." Some of my greatest teachers had "RN" after their names.

Environmental Racism

Many of the children who sought care at Kosair Children's Hospital during my years of medical practice were the children of poverty, a poverty often born out of racism, social injustice, discrimination, and the oft-ignored problem of environmental racism. And their medical problems often arose from their environment.

In our society we tend to place greater importance on comfort and wealth while ignoring what we are doing to the environment and the poor. So we place our environmental hazards in the backyards of the innocent poor, thereby diminishing their personhood and hastening their demise.

Toxins and dangerous chemicals from landfills, waste dumps, spills from trucks, and industrial emissions have all been cited as health risks. Proximity to major roadways is a factor in increasing rates of asthma. In fact, according to a recent article in the *Courier-Journal*, the west end of Louisville, the area where a large segment of the city's black population resides, has the city's poorest air quality. The same area has one of the highest rates of asthma.[2] The same article cites the need to create a buffer zone between schools and future major roadways. As I read this, I thought of our home on Brook Street in the 1950s with I-65 looming overhead as I walked out the front door. In the back of the house, the ramp from I-65 southbound to W. St. Catherine Street greeted me. From there I could look to my right and see the interstate within a few feet of Engelhard Elementary School.

The byproducts of industry, scientific and medical projects, and even agricultural processes all have the capability of being toxic, ignitable, corrosive, and/or reacting with other substances to become more dangerous. A variety of pesticides, such as dioxin, and solvents are released into the environment every day. Particulate pollution from incinerators, including hospital incinerators, accounts for a significant amount of toxins, especially mercury and dioxin. Many observers note the difficulty in knowing exactly what toxins are being released into the air, water, and earth. Meanwhile, research and monitoring has been patchy and not always well documented.

What is the health effect of environmental pollution? The most worrisome part is that we are not certain, but it cannot be good. From the standpoint of carcinogens, it may be years between exposure and clinical cancer or death.[3] Even worse, we are not always sure which toxins are being released, how much is being released, or what can be done to improve the situation.

What we do know is that in areas of increased pollution, asthma goes up significantly, leading to an increase in ER visits and hospitalizations. Not all of this can be explained by inadequate medical care and lack of compliance, although they do play a role. Increased blood lead levels are also noted, some of which can be explained by children chewing on the painted surfaces of old houses that are coated in lead-based paint. The poor are usually relegated to old houses. Most of the nearly four million children affected by lead poisoning in the United States each year are African American or Hispanic, living in urban areas.[4] We do know that lead causes central nervous system insults. What we don't know with certainty is what living with other toxins does to cognitive function in the developing child. Also, there is reasonable evidence that psychological depression and dysfunctional families increase in rate of occurrence and severity in areas of increased pollution and hazardous waste dumps.

In no way can justice be realized when one segment of the population is being bitten by rats, poisoned by toxic wastes, smothered by polluted air, and drowned in a sea of depression that is aggravated by the hopelessness of a victimized and dilapidated community. Justice requires that we as an inclusive community seek something better.

Who has benefited from toxic waste production? Considering the fact that it is often the byproduct of the manufacturing of things we use daily, WE DO! The products may be things for which we have a perceived need or, more often than not, we simply want and demand. Biomedical technology, which has improved our life span, has ironically contributed greatly to toxic waste that diminishes the lives of others. The destruction or altering of human habitat by highway and transportation technology, which benefits so many, can have its greatest negative impact on poor people of color. Our society seems to get more upset over a super highway destroying wetlands than about the destruction of a neighborhood, especially when that neighborhood is poor, black, or Hispanic. It seems that the ducks get more attention than the poor. The decision-makers, both public and private, simply are not well informed about health and racial issues in environmental planning.

In 1953 my grandmother and disabled uncle had moved into a third-floor apartment on 29th St. He had asthma and severe arthritis. Grandmother, though not in great health, was working in a laundry to support them, having been widowed one year earlier. Across the alley from their apartment was a creamery. The name sounds inviting, but vapors, noise, and milk in the streets were constant reminders that the neighborhood belonged to the creamery. Trains backed into the factory day and night, emitting smoke and bed-shaking vibrations. My uncle's asthma worsened. Sleep was difficult to come by. Vapor-covered sunlight was the order of the day. Why would they live there? Why not move? Because that is where they could afford to live. They were poor.

Such problems are compounded by the severe inattention given to them by people claiming adherence to a faith whose founder said, "Blessed are you who are poor, for yours is the kingdom of God" (Luke 6:20). Such news may come as a surprise to some uninformed wealthy folks who relegate the poor to live in the "kingdom of pollution." It is easy for us to forget that the poor are already limited in their boundaries, often prescribed by society as well as environmental issues. When further problems develop, there is a tendency in our society to blame, even demonize, the poor for their own victimization. When Hurricane Katrina went through New Orleans several years ago, thousands of poor, disproportionately black, were stranded. They were left on rooftops and highways and in the Super Dome. Incredibly, the media at times implied that was stupidity, laziness, or the desire to stay behind and commit crimes that prevented their leaving when, in fact, it was poverty and the lasting effects of longstanding systemic racism.

Poverty, in and of itself, with or without environmental racism, has an impact on our health in general and neurological disease in particular. In the early part of this century, it was reported that about thirty percent of children with disabilities lived in households with income below the federal poverty level as compared to sixteen percent without disabilities.[5] In a community where racism and social injustice has made it is mark, educational opportunities and job training are scarce. Even when there are jobs, there is most often racial bias in the marketplace so that people of color are "assigned" lower-paying jobs. Many find the circumstances overwhelming, even paralyzing, with resultant stress-related disorders and/or depression.

Poor parents of children with neurological disorders are less likely to be well informed. Access to specialists may be problematic due to transportation problems. Fear of costs adds to their frustration. Noncompliance and lack of follow-up are chronic problems. The family's poverty is increased by the costs of caregiving if, in fact, they can handle it at all. How does a mother work when she is caring for a significantly disabled child? Such problems need ongoing attention and our critical thinking that will hopefully produce some innovative ideas. However, the mood of our current society does not lend itself to compassion for the poor; rather society, more often than not, seeks to look for someone to blame—often the poor. Now, as a chaplain, I am even more aware of the adverse effect of such injustices on the spirit and psyche.

Injustice on Brook Street

All too often in the development of the community and other matters, the interests of the powerful are served with little or no regard for the poor and near-poor. For example, in 2008 when the poor of southwest Jefferson County, Kentucky, objected to the building of an explosive storage facility near their homes, I watched city officials wearing pinstriped suits say, in essence, "Well, we are going to build it anyway." Little regard was paid to the ill effect on the already devalued land of the working poor.

I am particularly sensitive to such due to the experiences of my childhood. Our family of six had moved to Brook Street in spring 1954. The Brook Street corridor was then part of an area in transition from a white middle-class neighborhood with a strong Jewish community to a lower-middle-class and blue-collar population. Most of those moving in were, like my family, low-income renters.

Our new dwelling place sat at the beginning of a row of houses dating to the turn of the century. The tree-lined street was itself a history lesson. Here and there, trolley tracks, long ago abandoned, broke through the asphalt worn thin by wheel after wheel. We were told that much of the tracks had been removed to use for military equipment during World War II. Barely could a late-1940s/early-1950s car park on either side along the leaf-filled curbs without risking a mirror or taillight. Twenty-five was the posted speed, but even in the early 1950s, driver illiteracy reigned.

We at first occupied the second floor of the south wing of a four-family unit. There were three rooms and a bath for our family of six. The living room was of good size, allowing space for our now-deteriorating gray sofa and chair, the kitchen chairs that had been banished from the kitchen for lack of space, and our 1951 RCA television with a twelve-inch screen, the first TV we had ever owned. My father told us that he had won "on the ponies" enough to pay cash for the TV. It was only later that I discovered how much he had lost in that enterprise.

In summer 1954 we moved to the apartment downstairs. It was the same as upstairs with two exceptions. First, but not foremost, a room had been made from the space under the stairs leading to the second floor. There, my brother and I had our bunk beds, while my sisters again shared a room with my parents. Second, and most important, was what my brother and I discovered in the only closet we had. The closet sat in a short hallway between the living room and bedroom. At the back of the closet was a panel of plywood that was easily removed to expose a dark, musty space. With the help of a flashlight, we could see dirt a few feet below and water pipes running in all directions. Then the scurrying of rats led to a quick closing of what we labeled the "secret passage." Well, we were not exactly heading for Narnia, but as eleven- and thirteen-year-olds do, we set out to see where we thought that passage led: the cellar.

The entrance to the cellar was guarded by two large, green wooden doors that lay at a forty-five-degree incline against the building just outside the kitchen door. My brother and I raised those doors and with some trepidation went down unpainted wooden steps to a cellar lined by dirt walls except for a few feet in the back where gray-stoned masonry produced a small fortress surrounding the boiler supplying steam to the radiators above. The cellar became a place of escape and discovery but mostly escape from noise and temperature extremes.

During the summer the apartment, particularly our little room, became intolerably hot. Sleep, always in short supply, came by moving my cotton-filled mattress to the front porch. The sounds and smells of those nights still linger in my mind. Bob's Little Tavern backed up to our apartment, sending our way the sounds of the jukebox and unintelligible shouting, mixed with the odor of stale beer being blown from the bar's exhaust fan. The space behind the tavern was also the depository for the waste products of the night's total consumption of beer. Despite the concoction of dissonant sounds and abhorrent smells, I did fall asleep eventually.

I awoke many mornings on that porch, but I will never forget one awakening, for it was to the sound of jackhammers and dump trucks. An invading army of heavy equipment was on its way north, its sole goal being the widening of Brook Street. The hoards had crossed Oak Street to occupy the 1000 block of Brook, just as Julius Caesar had crossed the Rubicon and Patton the Rhine, leaving a swath of destruction that Sherman would have envied. The trees were sacrificed, while the trolley tracks, once visible here and there, in one day's time became only a memory. By summer's end Brook Street was a sea of concrete walks and asphalt roads sailed by an armada of cars and trucks. By night came the disharmonious sounds of Bob's Little Tavern; by day came the growling and barking of Mack trucks, belching smoke as they headed north to Louisville's downtown. Noise became our constant companion.

In summer 1955 we moved a block away to Floyd near Oak Street. There, we had the whole house with a living room, dining room, and kitchen downstairs and three bedrooms up. Heaven! But that would not last even until Christmas as the government had purchased the house to make way for the North-South

Expressway, which later became part of I-65. President Eisenhower had pushed through the Federal Highway Act of 1956, also known as the National Interstate and Defense Highway Act. During the Cold War identifying about any project with national defense assured funding.[6] That which was intended to be defense for the nation became an offense to us. The initial Brook Street invasion now paled in the face of the new hoard of yellow Caterpillar earthmoving equipment. They came flattening the houses and piling layer upon layer of yellow-brown dirt on the once-tree-covered backyards and alleys. Block after block of houses were leveled on Floyd, St. Catherine, and Brook Streets, then hauled away, taking with them the reminders of afterschool front-porch visits, popsicles on a hot day in a friend's backyard, and spontaneous ballgames played anywhere possible. The giant earthmovers came, taking away our neighborhood and giving back only dirt, stone, concrete, and steel.

We moved back to Brook Street to the second floor of a wonderful old house. The foyer, all stained wood with intricate carving, spoke of former wealth and importance. My brother and I bunked in a small room just to the left of the stairwell from downstairs. The east-facing window was in a gable that stood out majestically, thus giving the external house a hint of richness that did not exist within. The early morning sun would often break through that window to greet me, at least until I-65 blocked the sunrise.

At the front of the apartment was the largest room. It was likely once the living room but now served as my parents' bedroom, as it offered the most privacy. It was separated from the center room by a sliding hardwood door. All the floors were of that same beautiful wood, now scratched and worn. The center room had likely been the dining room, but it became our living room, complete with a sofa, two soft gray chairs, but only one lamp with barely light enough for reading. Reading would have to find another venue. In the bathroom was a number-two washtub filled with the family's dirty clothes and covered with a faded red throw cover. Because there was a light over the sink adjacent to the tub, it became my "reading chair."

To the west through an extra-wide portal was a small eating area occupied by a table that could uncomfortably seat six, though it was no doubt designed for only four. There, my brother and I consumed our morning Cheerios or Wheaties while reading the cereal box and hoping we might collect enough Wheaties box tops to get whatever was being offered. Facsimiles of bills from the Confederate States of America were a sought-after commodity. "Save your Wheaties box tops; the South shall rise again" was the humor of the day. We collected a few Jefferson Davis bills but of course could spend none, and the South stayed put.

Victor H. Engelhard Elementary School, at one time the school of future civic leaders, including one mayor, faced south on Kentucky just west of Brook Street. An article in the *Filson Club History Quarterly* says the school "now served the rooming house and shifting population," resulting in Engelhard having the most turnover of pupils of any school in Louisville.[7] My family was among those "shifting." There, I attended the last few months of the fifth grade and all of the sixth under the tutelage of Mrs. Alice Laidley.

Old wooden floors with indentions in the boards marked our third-floor classrooms. There was a distinctive but indescribable odor that, even now, I would recognize blindfolded. The blackboards were still black then, not green or white. I visited there a few years ago. It is now the Heuser Hearing Center. The wood and the blackboards have not changed in appearance or smell.

Cleaning the fire escape was the most memorable part of my sixth-grade year. The fire escape was a silo-like structure attached to the east side of the school. If needed, the students would exit a door and slide down a spiraling metal tube to safety. That great sliding board the teachers called the fire escape had to be cleaned weekly by sitting on a burlap bag and sliding down three floors to the ground. We took turns at that duty. If some anxious soul showed reluctance, my hand would go up immediately. Fire drills were a cause for celebration.

In the second half of the 1950s, I-65 was built diagonally across the intersection of Brook and Kentucky Streets within a few yards of Engelhard Elementary School, a building that dates back to 1886. The ramp to St. Catherine Street started just past Engelhard School and continued through our backyard. The configuration effectively placed our home in a triangle of steel, concrete, and exhausts. The school fared no better. The school playground, the site of many a kickball game, was now under the interstate. The fire-escape silo had to come down. The North-South Expressway, the designation for I-65 at that time, had effectively made the building useless for educational purposes.[8]

I left my Brook Street home in fall 1961 to enroll at Vanderbilt University. With me went the gnawing memories of a neighborhood severely altered and nearly destroyed by careless planning and an unwitting city and state leadership.

In spring 2007 I stopped my pickup truck on East Kentucky Street just north of Brook Street. I surveyed the remains of what was our family's backyard in the 1950s. Gray concrete pillars, now cracking from a half century of winters and the continuous flow of vehicles above, arose from the ground like gravestones, marking what was but is no longer. Over a wire fence, rusting and bent, and up an incline to the furthest nook of steel and concrete were small piles of rags or clothes, an unoccupied mattress, and two sleeping figures. It was home for the homeless.

The house on the southwest corner of Brook and Kentucky Street had been demolished to make room for I-65 and an exit ramp. The remainder of the houses on the west side of the block had their backyards reduced to about fifty feet of grass or gravel, giving each home an up-close spectacular view of the asphalt river flowing to St. Catherine Street. The interstate sign above would read "St. Catherine West," making mention of neither the humanity sleeping below nor the memories buried there.

I wanted to call out to the sleeping strangers, but I decided to respect their privacy and wait for another day to introduce myself. Had I awakened them, I would have told them how special is the place they had chosen. I would tell them there once was a sycamore tree and a giant rambling rosebush nearby that offered shade in the heat of the summer. Had they dropped by then, I would have offered to share the cool of that spot where I sat and read books and petted our dog, Prince, as he, tired from chasing after sticks and a ball, panted in the summer heat. Prince was just a dog, no brand name. He had short black hair with a white left front foot and a streak of white on his nose. My brother and I had found him wandering the alley one day. After he was offered food and water, he decided to stay.

I would tell the homeless strangers that somewhere under that mound of concrete and steel are Prince's remains. Something had happened to that wiry acrobat who could catch a ball in midair with an accuracy that might bring envy from Mickey Mantle. I am not sure what that something was. We buried him near the tree in the backyard, marking his grave with a few old bricks found in the alley. The tree and overgrown rosebush that provided relief from the summer sun and a barrier from the alley traffic became Prince's grave marker. He would have liked the idea of his place of eternal repose becoming a refuge for others displaced by life.

I recall a children's book, *The Little House*, a story of a house that experiences loneliness and sadness as the city grows up around it. It is towed away from its birthplace as tall buildings and highways surround it.[9] The house we occupied could not be towed. It stands today as the second house from Kentucky Street on the west side of Brook, though it sits on the third lot, as the first house had succumbed to the wrecking ball. I do not know if the house on Brook Street is sad now, but I am saddened every time I drive past it. I am reminded of an injustice done to a neighborhood, my family, and me.

Moving On or Evicted?

It can be concluded readily from what I have written so far that my family moved frequently. I was never quite sure why we were moving. I assumed then that my parents had found a better place to live; perhaps I was correct—some of the time. I have no recollection of where my family lived when I was born. I know it was an apartment in the 200 block of East Broadway, but that is about it. The first "home" I recall was on Indiana Avenue (now Belmar) across from East Audubon Baptist Church. The four rooms and a sun porch plus a bath with a tub but no hot water were luxurious compared to what was to come. We had to move because the building was being destroyed to make room for expansion and parking for a hardware owned by our landlord.

For the next few months we lived in the front two rooms of a house built for one family at the corner of Sherman and Taylor Avenues in the Camp Taylor neighborhood, a remainder of a World War I training camp for the U.S. Army. There was a flagpole in the front yard, leading us to believe the house had at one time been important, perhaps the home of a high-ranking officer. We never received confirmation of such, but the idea made us feel better about how we were living. We shared a bathroom with the owners, who lived in the back bedroom and the kitchen. Our family of six bedded down in three beds crammed into the front room. What made this a good place to live was the presence of three boys next door and one more across the street. Some bonds were made then that have persisted to this day. The strongest bond was to the mother of the three boys next door, Mrs. Dorothy Dunn. She was the one who barred me from their yard for cursing and then invited me to church and Sunday school and to a boys group that met in their basement. That may well have been my first real experience with grace. It was there in the Dunn's home that I first encountered prayer (I will tell the rest of the story in ch. 10 when I talk about prayer). Suffice it to say for now that even though we were living uncomfortably in two rooms, I had found a caring community next door. Then we moved. I was nearly six years old.

Our home on Fern Valley Road consisted of three rooms, an outhouse, and a sulfa water well with a pump. A coal-burning stove in the kitchen heated the three small rooms. The nearest neighbor lived across the road and down a long driveway. I was never invited, so I never walked that driveway. Community came in the form of my first-grade class at Okolona Elementary. But even that did not last. When the snow melted and spring was near, we moved to a house down the street from the Dunn family. Four rooms and a bath! But still no hot running water. We stayed put there until the end of fourth grade. I was a frequent visitor in the Dunn home. I often tried to get myself invited to meals, and it worked. All the family, eventually six boys and a girl, were gathered around the table. It was crowded, but I was given a seat; I had a community of acceptance away from the intermittent problems at home prompted by alcoholism and all that goes with that disease. There is no greater community-building activity than sitting down at a common table. But this would not last long.

At the end of fourth grade, my mother announced that we were moving to Okolona to a house with four rooms and hot running water. At last we had made it! A hot bath whenever I wanted was something I had never had. Then we moved again. This time we were again sharing a home with the owners. They slept upstairs, and we had downstairs. All else was shared. Several months later I came home from school, having just won a book in the fifth-grade spelling bee, and found everything was packed up. The next morning we moved to Brook Street. In total we lived in eleven different places before I left for college at age seventeen. I had never become attached to a place called "home."

For many who are "moving on," it is not a choice. For the poor the threat of loss of a place to call "home" is real. In the early part of this century, I arrived in the hospital parking lot at 6 a.m. Doctors' parking spaces are right at the beginning of the parking garage. I knew which cars would be there when I arrived. The pediatric neurosurgeon and the chief of pediatric anesthesiology were almost always there in their usual spots. Any aberrant vehicle was quickly noticed. On this particular morning an old tan Buick occupied the last space in the physicians' lot. Not far away was a sign threatening removal of illegally parked cars.

A man was leaning against the window, obviously asleep. As I approached the car, I saw three more figures in the back lying on boxes of clothes. The floor of the car was strewn with fast-food bags and cups. I immediately recognized them as the father and siblings of my critically ill epileptic patient. Over the next few minutes I learned that this old car was "home" and had been for several months. They had been evicted from their small house in an outlying county with a significant poverty rate. Eviction is much more common among the poor, therefore more common among African Americans.

By day's end, with the help of our social worker and several nurses, the family had a temporary place to live about a mile from the hospital. Over the next few days I learned about the effect homelessness had on the children and my patient. The lack of rest and adequate nutrition has an adverse effect on intractable epilepsy. How does a child get well from anything while living in the family car?

A few years ago I started working with the reading program at Engelhard School where I attended from the end of fifth grade through the entire sixth grade. The school sits in one of the poorest zip codes in Kentucky. The principal was a compassionate woman who knew the living conditions of her students. At the beginning of school, she took her faculty on a tour of the neighborhoods where the students lived. But how do we take a tour of the dwelling places of the homeless? Fourteen entering students were homeless. Some were in shelters for homeless families. Several students were living in the family car. Have you ever done your homework while holding a flashlight or parked under a streetlight?

Harvard sociologist Matthew Desmond has published a forceful book on the impact of eviction in America. He sees a stable home as the focal point of our lives, for it is there that we have the possibility of escaping the pressure of day-to-day work and having time to just be ourselves. The home is "the wellspring of personhood," the place where we begin to learn about community and the value of working for the common good. It is home where we initially establish our identity.[10] There also is the potential for some sense of security. When frequent moves are made, especially forced moves, things change. Not only is there a loss of whatever stability might exist in a family; there is also a loss of a sense of belonging, as schools and neighborhoods are left behind. Such was the case for me as my family migrated from dwelling to dwelling over a period of seventeen years. Those who live in comfortable middle- or upper-class neighborhoods will not be able to relate to what I am talking about, as frequent moving for financial reasons, including eviction, is the province of the poor.

When we saw children with neurologic conditions in our clinic, we had to be sensitive to the psychological sequelae of the instability of place. Having a poor self-image or being outright depressed was not uncommon. It is little wonder that caregivers looked worn out, dismayed, and bewildered. Often they were ashamed of what was happening to them and their families.

The Church and the Mobile Poor

As a chaplain I try be aware of the negative spiritual impact of having no permanent place to call "home." The support of a church community can be central, but it is often lacking, as the family is not in any one place long enough to establish lasting relationships with anyone, let alone the local church. Movement within the same general neighborhood of two blocks of Brook Street and a block away on Floyd afforded me the opportunity to become part of a church community that sustained and enriched my life and the lives of two of my siblings. This came about largely through the efforts of one church staff member and several dedicated laypersons. It wasn't so much programs and big money, nor was it entertaining worship services (but we had some of that). Walnut Street Baptist Church (WSBC) was so named because it had its beginning at Fourth and Walnut Streets. When the church moved east in the first decade of the twentieth century to Third and St. Catherine Streets in what was then the suburbs, it took its name with it. Walnut Street is now Muhammad Ali Street.

One of the most significant encounters in my life took place in our living room in summer 1955. I had attempted to scale the fence on our side yard. In those days some fences had sharp projections, almost like barbed wire, that these days are bent for safety reasons. Just as I thought I was clearing the fence, I impaled my right arm on one of the barbs. I freed my extremity but had sustained a three-inch laceration on the anterior surface of my forearm. As I entered our apartment, I was already feeling lightheaded. I stretched out on the couch, barely hearing my mother's lecture on such foolishness, foolishness that would now cost us a trip to the Norton Hospital, which was then at the corner of Third and Oak Streets.

As I rested on the sofa, there was a knock on the door. Two bald men in suits and ties stood in our doorway. Mother let them into our house, an act that would set the course of my life for years to come. They were laymen, not church staff members, from WSBC. "We have come to invite your family to Sunday school and church," they said to my mother. Mother, hardly hearing or understanding their words, replied, "Talk to Billy here. He needs something." Then came the offer, "Come to Sunday school at least twice per month and you can play on the church basketball or softball team." And I, on the verge of either passing out or vomiting, agreed with the plan. They said a prayer and exited. Later, I would see them in the same light as the visitors to Abraham's tent who came as messengers, setting the course of his journey. Over the span of the next fifty-two years at WSBC, I was baptized, learned to study Scripture and pray, ordained a deacon, taught Sunday school for thirty years, and experienced a call to ministry, a call that further determined the course of my life. To this day I do not know the identity of those two visitors. If I were again allowed admission to that room, I would take off my shoes, for I would be standing on holy ground.

I started attending the church and its Sunday school in the in the summer of my eleventh year. At first I attended Sunday school and church for the fellowship and to be able to play on the church athletic teams. What a combo: God and basketball! To this day I value church activity programs for bringing kids off the street and into the church. Through the influence of the church youth director, Mary Miller, church became more than fun and fellowship. She led me to grow spiritually though prayer and Scripture study. How old-fashioned can you be!

Mary Miller was unique. Born in China to missionaries, she signed on as the church secretary after a World War II army career. She became deeply concerned about the youth of the church when the youth pastor left. She took on the task of ministering to the youth though she had no specific training for the job, just passion and compassion. Her greatest passion seemed to be for the "neighborhood kids," especially for those who had no family involvement in the church. Most days after school, ten to fifteen of us would gather around her office at the front of the chapel where we had study hall combined with prayer and Scripture reading. It was there I first read Psalm 139, which I still read often or quote to myself as I seek to know the heart of God. Even today I hear Mary Miller praying aloud and admonishing me to behave and study. Little wonder that our youth group referred to her as "Mother Mary."

I am not sure who my first Sunday school teacher was, but the first one I recall is Mr. Charles Sell. Every Sunday, without fail, Mr. Sell sat down to a small wooden desk and opened his Bible and his Sunday School Quarterly, so called because the Southern Baptist Sunday School Board in Nashville published via the Broadman Press weekly Bible lessons on a quarterly basis. He would then begin to tell a Bible story with a life lesson for the week.

I recall very little of what Mr. Sell said. I recall no fancy theological words or exegetical discourses. The first and perhaps only lesson I remember is the story of Joseph and his many-colored robe. The image of a rainbow-colored garment emblazed on the front of the glossy publication did leave a lasting impression. More importantly, I will never forget the man, Charles Sell, who faithfully arrived every Sunday morning and sat down to study the Bible with a half-dozen boys. As far as I know, he did so long before and long after my year under his tutelage.

Every Sunday Mr. Sell was dressed in a suit and tie; his hair, already gray as I recall, was forever neatly in place. Once our youth group made a trip to the Kentucky Baptist headquarters in Middletown. The *Western Recorder*, the Kentucky Baptist newspaper, was printed there in those days. There also was my teacher, Mr. Sell, dressed in a printer's apron and setting the print type for the paper by hand. He looked as neat as he did on Sunday, even wearing a tie as I recall. With a gentle smile he greeted each of us by name. What he was doing immediately resonated with me, for in those days typesetting was offered as an elective class in middle school. I was one who "elected" to learn the trade but only for one semester.

When I was a preteen and teen, the face of the church was not ordained clergy so much as dedicated laypersons who looked beyond the outward signs of poverty and the questionable behavior of young people growing up under the adverse circumstances of poverty and dysfunctional families. There were many who impacted my life in my teens. Seminary students gave freely of their time. As volunteers they coached church athletic teams, acted as camp counselors, and taught Bible classes. There were working parents and grandparents who faithfully taught us on Sunday and Wednesday nights. Some invited the youth group into their homes on Saturday or Sunday evening for fellowship and Bible study. I would like to say it was the Bible study that drew me there, but more often than not, it was the girls who prompted my loyal attendance. Nonetheless, I did join in the study, and I did learn.

What I mean to say in all this story-telling is that the response of the church to the unsettled and migratory family dealing with poverty, injustice, and homelessness should be love as manifested in community-building, teaching, and developing lasting relationships. No easy task—perhaps even harder for wealthy churches, which have a tendency to remain rather homogeneous.

The poor do not command a hearing from the wealthy or those in power (see Prov 18:23). The Brook Street neighborhood was nearly destroyed by the construction of an expressway, as were other neighborhoods in Louisville's west end, but no one asked how our families, the working poor, felt about it. Little regard was paid to the ill effect on the already devalued properties of the working poor. The sages must have seen similar activity, as Proverbs 13:23 notes how the property of the poor is unjustly "swept away," making self-support more difficult. It is not unusual that on "the side of the oppressors there was power" (Eccl 4:1). Job also saw that the "powerful possess the land" (Job 22:8). Uncaring powers often keep the weak and poor from realizing their full God-given potential.

Compassion, the prerequisite for doing and seeking justice, has not been the hallmark of the powers-that-be. There has been a prevalent unwillingness to listen to the cry of the poor, not to mention their wisdom. If the wealthy, including those in power, do not listen, then they are better able to sleep, enjoy the Derby, and guard their wealth. Poverty is out of sight and out of mind. Perhaps the rich and powerful oppose justice for the poor because justice demands the sharing of wealth.

Migrant Farmworkers in Brief

I know very little about migrant workers, but I do know someone who does. Seth M. Holmes, Ph.D., M.D., wrote the winner of the 2014 Margaret Mead Award.[11] Holmes lived and worked with the people in the mountains of Oaxaca and in the camps of migratory workers. His book, *Fresh Fruit, Broken Bodies: Migrant Farmworkers in the United States*,[12] has and will open one's eyes and heart to a segment of America that escapes the view of most of us. I highly recommend this book.

A Call to Advocacy[13]

Several years ago I met Sally Jane as she walked into a clinic pushing her severely impaired granddaughter in a wheelchair. Sally Jane had become Melissa's caregiver when her mother abandoned her, no longer able to cope with the daily behavior problems and seizures. Sally Jane had only an eighth-grade education, lived in a mobile home, and had no health insurance. Having received plenty of well-meaning advice about how to "fix" her granddaughter, Sally Jane carried a bag of herbs and vitamins a friend had helped her purchase on the Internet. She had also heard about a place in Florida treating children like Melissa with hyperbaric oxygen. It was not an approved treatment for her condition, but this did not faze her.

Medicaid covered her granddaughter's medical expenses, but Sally Jane struggled to find adequate medical care for herself. Respite care for Melissa was scarce. Even the best efforts of the social worker could not overcome the enormity of the problems of poverty or the lack of education, income, and health insurance. Under intolerable stress, Sally Jane's health deteriorated, culminating in her untimely death at the age of fifty-five.

According to Luke's Gospel, the story of Jesus' birth was announced to poor shepherds keeping watch over their flock. A shepherd otherwise engaged risks the life or health of her sheep. Similarly, we are called to be aware of what is happening outside the walls of the church, the clinic, and the hospital because that is where sheep are often found. But how can healthcare professionals and the church make a unique contribution? What can or should we do beyond the care we provide professionally? Allow me to offer a few recommendations:

1. Be an educator! Guidance is needed as your faith community members and patients face changes in healthcare delivery, often reimbursement-driven. Formularies will change or be reduced. In addition, a plethora of claims for the effectiveness of this or that treatment greets them on the Internet. Websites look official, but few are peer-reviewed. As a rule of thumb, as advertisements on a website go up, trustworthiness goes down. Medical school and hospital websites are usually more reliable.

2. Be an advocate for the poor and middle income. Income and education level have been factors in health outcomes throughout history. Life expectancy

is significantly longer for men and women in the highest income brackets. Today, it is not just the very poor who are having bad health outcomes, but also those in the large and ever-growing middle class.

3. Be an advocate for education for low- and middle-income children. Keep in mind that the way to better income is tied heavily to education. Public health literature documents great health disparities at various levels of education. The lack of a high school diploma or equivalent is associated with being three times more likely than a college graduate to die before age sixty-five.

Schools need volunteers to help with tutoring students in reading. Several years ago the *Reading Is Fundamental* program was cut from the federal budget. This program provided free books for children to take home as their own. Ever see a child get excited over owning her own copy of a *Junie B. Jones* book? Reading is foundational for success in school and in the job market, both of which will more likely mean "healthcare coverage."

4. Be an advocate for minorities and immigrants. Minority status is statistically associated with lower levels of education, income, healthcare access and outcomes. There is no simple one-to-one correlation. Employment, wealth, neighborhood characteristics, and social policies, as well as culture, health beliefs, and country of origin all come into play. The church is called to a ministry of hospitality and welcoming the stranger.

The task we are given is not easy, but we can make a difference.

Notes

[1] Bob Herbert, "Poor, Black, and Dumped On," *Courier-Journal*, October 6, 2006, section A, 16.

[2] James Bruggers, "Hot Zones for Asthma Mapped," *Courier-Journal*, June 28, 2017, section A, 1.

[3] Peter S. Wenz, "Environmental Health," in *Encyclopedia of Bioethics*, 3rd Edition, ed. Stephen Garrard Post (New York: MacMillan Academic. 2003) 777–78.

[4] Rebecca Todd Peters, *In Search of the Good Life: The Ethics of Globalization* (New York: Continuum, 2004), 114–15.

[5] J. William Holmes, "The Impact of Poverty on Neurological Disease," pediatric grand rounds, Kosair Children's Hospital, January 6, 2007.

[6]H. W. Brands, *American Dreams: The United States Since 1945* (New York: Penguin, 2011), 82.

[7]Sam V. Noe, "The Louisville Public Schools: Their Names, Their History," *Filson Club History Quarterly* 38 (July 1964): 53.

[8]Ibid.

[9]Virginia Lee Burton, *The Little House*, 60th anniversary ed. (Boston: Houghton-Mifflin, 1978).

[10]Matthew Desmond, *Evicted: Poverty and Profit in the American City* (New York: Broadway Books, 2017), 293.

[11]Seth Holmes is no kin to me. He is the son of my college roommate, Dr. Edwin R. Holmes III.

[12]*Fresh Fruit, Broken Bodies: Migrant Farmworkers in the United States* (Berkeley: University of California Press, 2013).

[13]Bill Holmes, "Interfacing: Who Will Keep Watch Over the Flock?," Church Health Reader, accessed August 31, 2017, http://www.chreader.org/will-keep-watch-flock/. Used with permission.

CHAPTER 9

Racism

City of My Youth
By Houston A. Baker Jr.[1]

A seed-time of quick violence
And hours resonant with despair.
Growing in this southern town
Was against the law,
Each green shot lopped off...

There was no sunshine six days a week;
On Sunday it beamed for ecstatic religion, and
Settled at dusk to a blood-red and sinful sky.

Finding my way through texts on family shelves,
I talked of Candide and Copernicus
To the stunned horror of others,
Became prey to charges of literacy
As hooked knives of the South swung low
To carry me home:
Black sufferers demanded my head
(on a platter)
And white women hinted worse.

Through this spawning time I read on, praying
For a moment to confide its truth,
In later hours ringing with despair,
To engage the burden of literacy (thank God!)
In the open air.

Highland Baptist Church
(a cross for every homicide in Louisville the past year)

Thoughts of a Guilty Bystander

When I pull up a chair and listen to the story of one now facing a critical illness or death, I endeavor to recognize the wholeness of that person. All of his life experiences come to bear on the moment. He does not exist simply as a case of this or that in a vacuum or a specimen in a jar. No child's illness or the course of his neurologic problems exists free of all the ramifications of place, race, family income, and education level. I have discussed the impact of environmental racism and poverty. Where a child lives contributes to her ongoing health status. Historically, and still so today, living circumstances are significantly influenced by racism. I became acutely aware of this as I cared for children from central and western Kentucky as well as southern Indiana. This same racism historically has played a major role in the education of our children both in terms of place and quality.

In 1954 the U.S. Supreme Court handed down a decision in the case of Brown v. the Topeka Board of Education. As an eleven-year-old kid I was more interested in making a jumpshot than with whom I would attend school. I doubt I gave any thought to the changes coming in the Louisville Public Schools, changes that prompted some concern among white parents, and, as I understand, among some black parents as well. In compliance with the ruling, in 1956 I started eighth grade at the newly integrated Manly Junior High School. For the most part there were no problems in terms of violence or verbal abuse. The problems were more in the attitudes of some administrators, teachers, and students. The outward expressions of these attitudes toward black students were not always out there for all to see. Even when seen, they might not have been recognized for what they were. Unfairness toward black students went unchallenged.

In fall 1957 my African-American classmate Beverly Neal (Watkins) and I were "horsing around" in our homeroom class. I ended up with a lead pencil poked into the palm of my left hand. I do not recall the poke so much as the first time I looked at my palm and saw a tiny black spot of graphite. I don't recall either of us being angry. I do recall reminding her and telling everyone else about it at nearly every reunion.

Beverly and I revisited those days over coffee not long ago. She says she does not recall the reason for the pencil poke but does recall the hurt and anger of those days. The schools may have been desegregated, but the hearts and minds of white students, teachers, and administrators were something less than open and loving. We as students were together in the same space but not the same spirit. There was little in the way of community that extended beyond the walls of the school. Racial equality was hard to come by.

That pencil lead still shows. We laugh about it from time to time. That small speck in the palm of my left hand has served to remind me of things as they were but should not have been. That marker from another time in my life causes me to say, "Yes, Beverly, I think I also would have been hurt and angry." As for me, I wish I had been more perceptive of what was going on in the lives of my classmates.

The inequities were obvious to those who were paying attention; I was not. Classmate Raoul Cunningham, now president of the Louisville chapter of the NAACP, would later say he rejected the notion of an integrated college because of his experiences at Louisville Male High School (LMHS).[2] I was inexcusably unaware of the discrimination occurring all around me. I do recall sensing that something was not quite right. Being consumed by my own struggles with near poverty and the desire to achieve academic success—you see, I am already making excuses.

I managed to keep whatever concerns I had about racial injustice and the "integration that wasn't" comfortably at the back of my mind for years, pushing back those memories of 1956–1961 every time they sought my attention. One thing did keep popping up at each of our high school reunions; our school yearbook, *The Bulldog*, received its every-five-year review, serving as a reminder of the reality of segregation within what we called a "desegregated" school. There were no black class officers and few, if any, honors noted for black students. Additionally, there were no black teachers. Desegregated? Perhaps. Integrated? Absolutely not!

In early 2001 the *New York Times Book Review* had a brief reference to a book by Professor Houston A. Baker Jr. of Duke University. My classmate had written *Turning South Again: Re-thinking Modernism/Rereading Booker T.* Having no idea what the book was about, I ordered it from Amazon. I will never forget my initial reading of the first twenty pages. I was about to rethink my own complicity in the segregation of black students at the "desegregated" LMHS. Baker begins several of his publications with accounts of his youth in Louisville, a youth much different than my own. Though the schools were "desegregated," black people were still excluded from full participation in the life of the school as well as the community as a whole. More often than not, they were on the outside looking in.[3]

Soon after reading Baker's work, I shared it at our fortieth reunion. I apologized to the black members of our class. I also read aloud from his book. Word got back to Houston in Nashville, where he was a distinguished university professor at Vanderbilt. We communicated by email several times over the next few years. Finally, we got together in March 2007. Along with our wives, we met at the Tin Angel restaurant near the Vanderbilt campus in Nashville. It was for me a profound healing moment. I believe it was so for Houston as well.

Other than my memories and those of my fellow black students, is there "hard" evidence that black students were not truly integrated into the local public schools from 1956–1961? Yes, they were in the classrooms, on the athletic teams, in the same lunchroom, and in the same gymnasium. However, with even a cursory look through the publications from Manly Junior High and the *Brook n' Breck*, the school newspaper for LMHS, it is clear that black students did not experience the same school life white students enjoyed. There is very little about black students and their achievements unless they were highly successful athletes. One black athlete once informed me that he as a gifted athlete knew he had received a pass, an exemption. Among the white students he was one of the most liked students.

I will not go through each publication and newspaper column by column. Suffice it to say that there was a dearth of attention given to black students. Most stories are about white students and their accomplishments. The school newspaper had no black writers. The yearbook staff was all white. The class officers were all white. With a few exceptions, the "Senior Superlatives," the senior students with the most of this or that, were all white.

When we celebrated our fiftieth reunion, we asked Houston Baker to be the keynote speaker. The following excerpt accurately captures the truth of our life together at LMHS:

> On that Male High School election day, we assembled in the auditorium to choose officers for our class of 1961. All the black students sat in the auditorium as a completely segregated constituency. We did not sit alone because we thought or declared ourselves "exclusive." We sat alone because none of our white fellows joined us. And so we had devised a plan. Since we were so outnumbered, our best strategy was to choose just one remarkably outstanding black student as our candidate for election. We, of course, chose Raoul Cunningham. Raoul was Male's most prized debater. He was a valued officer in ROTC. He was a first-rate and beloved student. He was a citizen activist of Louisville, putting his life on the line for civil rights to bring social justice to America. We black students watched, unbelieving, as across the aisles and before and behind us on every side, our white classmates refused Raoul even a minor post in student governance.
>
> We as a group nominated Raoul for each office on the roster as the calls for nominations proceeded from highest to lowest. Raoul—which is to say *we*—lost every bid for inclusion. I did not know how to process what happened that day. For me the auditorium and the election were as terrible in my memory during the 1993 tour as they had been more than three decades before. In 1993 the cruelty of racial privilege and its crushing disregard for merit were still a vicious assault on my person. I knew by then that an absence of knowledge and the harm that such

ignorance imposes on others does not lessen the trauma of those of us who are hurt for life. "I didn't know" never serves as a sufficient mantra for reconciliation and healing. And no shame is greater than when adult administrators, teachers, guidance counselors, or coaches knowingly engage in racialized language and acts that harm children.[end]

A few years ago a historical marker was dedicated to the civil rights protestors of spring 1961. Thanks to Brown v. Board of Education, many were my classmates at LMHS. While I as a white student enjoyed my junior and senior years at the "desegregated" LMHS, my black classmates were being arrested for trying to sit at a lunch counter or restaurant table in downtown Louisville. However, Beverly Neal Watkins says she missed class only once due to her civil rights activities. Another fellow student once told me his arrest record started in Louisville and continued at Howard University and beyond. No one at LMHS, neither our teachers nor administrators, spoke a word about the struggle going on downtown. It was as though some of my black classmates were invisible.

I and other white students were aware of the absence of our black classmates, but I did not then grasp the magnitude of what was happening. They were being arrested for sitting in restaurants that might welcome me. In doing so they were changing the course of Louisville's history. They probably would not claim the title, but they are heroes. They also caused me to see my own racism.

My LMHS classmates—Beverly Neal Watkins, Emma Foust Smith, James Bryant, Lawrence H. Williams, Raoul Cunningham, Franklin Jones, Kirk Bright, Jeff Alston, Houston A. Baker Jr., and others—changed forever who I am and how I see the world. I trust they have affected many more. As I salute my black high school classmates, I ask others and myself, "Who are we excluding today from full participation in society? What prejudices do we harbor? Who will be today's heroes?"

Today, two factors—the threat of gun violence and mass incarceration of black men—loom large in black lives, impacting them psychologically, physically, and spiritually. The year we graduated from high school, 1961, President John F. Kennedy initiated what was then called an "anti-delinquency" program in several cities. Black neighborhoods were targeted. The stated purpose was to educate and put black people to work and thereby reduce crime. The program was later expanded by Lyndon Johnson and became known as the "war on poverty." Johnson and then Nixon instituted a program that led to the increased arrest and imprisonment of both black and white urban youth. At one point there was targeting of black urban youth who had relatives with arrest records. The so-called war on poverty became a war on crime—and a war on young black men. So great were the arrests that prison builders made a handsome profit.[4] Today, African Americans, without respect to the income and social standing, are imprisoned more than any racial group in America.[5] One significant result of mass incarceration has been "felon disenfranchisement," as convicted felons come out of prison without any voting rights.[6] While this is being addressed in some states, such as Kentucky, it remains a significant problem, especially for black men. To some extent community involvement and the election of more African-American representatives will have a mitigating effect on the never-ending injustice facing African Americans in general but black men in particular.

I have listened with a heavy heart as young black women and men express fear of seeing their sons gunned down on the street in a drive-by shooting or, in some cases, by law-enforcement officers. A record 123 homicides were reported in Louisville in 2016. The number for 2017 is so far threatening to exceed last year. A disproportionate number of the homicide victims are black. Each year Highland Baptist Church of Louisville places small wooden crosses in the churchyard, representing each homicide victim. This is done as a part of worship with the members carrying crosses from the front of the sanctuary to a grassy area out front. The crosses are hammered into the ground one by one. It is sobering and sad to hear the constant hammering over a period of fifteen to twenty minutes. Meanwhile, the congregants pray and reflect.[7]

Notes

[1] Houston A. Baker Jr., *Spirit Run* (Detroit: Lotus Press, 1982). 11. Reprinted by permission of author.

[2] Tracy E. K'Meyer, *From* Brown *to* Meredith*: The Long Struggle for School Desegregation in Louisville, Kentucky, 1954–2007* (Chapel Hill: University of North Carolina Press, 2013), 78.

[3] Houston A. Baker Jr., *Turning South Again: Re-thinking Modernism, Re-reading Booker T.* (Durham: Duke University Press, 2001), 16.

[4] Elizabeth Hinton, *From the War on Poverty to the War on Crime: The Making of Mass Incarceration in America* (Cambridge: Harvard University Press, 2016), 3–4.

[5] Ibid., 5.

⁶Ibid., 336.

⁷There have been several excellent, eye-opening books on mass incarceration of black men. In addition to Elizabeth Hinton's excellent work cited above, Michelle Alexander of Ohio State University has written a *New York Times* bestseller, *The New Jim Crow: Mass Incarceration in the Age of Colorblindness* (New York: New Press, 2012). Both books are must-reads for all of us.

CHAPTER 10

Prayer

And What Shall We Say to God?

If you have been around church for a long time, especially if you grew up in a fairly conservative evangelical church as I did, prayer stories abound. Likewise, if you have been around critical illness, dying, and death for very long, and tried to do the work of a pastor or chaplain, you will likely have become a person of prayer.

Having said this, I have a strong suspicion that for many prayer is more something we talk about than something we do on a regular basis. To be sure, we all have prayers that we recite from time to time. Nearly every Christian knows at least part of the Lord's Prayer. There are also those prayers that contain the ritualized language of our particular faith group.

In the church of my youth, the pastor, without warning, would call on a deacon to do the offertory prayer or even the benediction. It was remarkable how much the prayers sounded so much alike from week to week. There were acceptable words and phrases that essentially had been unwittingly made a part of the unofficial liturgy of the church. Nonetheless, such prayers became something of a teaching tool and to some extent presented an answer to the question "What do I say to God?"

When I was eight years old, I was invited to our neighbor's home for a Royal Ambassadors meeting, a Southern Baptist Church boys group. I recall spending a lot of time hearing about the work of missionaries such as Lottie Moon and William Carey. One particular gathering is forever burned into my memory circuits. We were asked by the leader to form a circle and then, in turn, offer a "sentence of prayer." For sure there had been no time in my life up to that point where I had publicly uttered anything that even remotely resembled a prayer. In fact, at one point I had been banned from the yard and very house in which I stood that night because I had repeatedly used profanity as we played in the front yard. Before my time to pray came, I leaned over and whispered into the ear of my friend, "Gary, what do I say?" I received no answer, and I have no recollection of what I said when my turn came. I do recall what Gary said to me after the prayer circle ended: "Billy, never speak aloud when people are praying; God might not hear them." It was then I recalled what I heard in the prayers that night: "Be with the missionaries in China, the soldiers in Korea, and with everyone who is sick." Beyond feeling that God was about to be very busy, I was left with uncertainty about what to say to God. I still have some uncertainty about what to say, but I am okay with that now. I am more interested in hearing what God has to say to me—not an easy task, as I have a somewhat noisy heart.

Prayer was a big part of my youth group experience as a teenager at WSBC. Being a downtown or inner-city kid, I often met with other teens at the front of the chapel near the office of our youth minister, Mary Miller, the daughter of missionaries to China and herself a former officer in the Women's Army Corp. Mary had come to the church to be a secretary/clerk, but she saw a need that had to be filled and then did so. Mary would read some Scripture or have us read it; then she would ask us to spend some time in silent prayer before ending with her own prayer for us. I often heard her pray, "Speak to us, Lord Jesus, that we might hear and know you." If there was much in the way of "Lord, help Billy with his homework" or "Help these boys and girls make good grades," I don't recall it. The emphasis I recall was on hearing and understanding. Afterward, we scattered out over the chapel to do our homework, using a pew for a desk. We gathered again later to pray. After forming a circle of sorts on two pews with the front-row kids turning around on their knees, we were asked to pray aloud as we felt led. Mary Miller suggested that we each verbalize what was "weighing on our hearts." I don't recall what I said, but I do recall being very concerned about revealing my deepest concerns to my peers. Long silences filled the time between our verbalized prayers. I always wondered why we lingered in the silence of the chapel for what seemed like eternity. Now, years later, I know it was so I might hear God.

In the Sermon on the Mount, Jesus said, "Pray, then, in this way." Mention the Lord's Prayer in a room full of Christians of different stripes, and you will get immediate looks of recognition. But sometimes I get the feeling that it stops right there. The kingdom most often prayed for in much of American Christianity is modeled more after our political and social agendas, not the kingdom of God. The will we seem to be most interested in is our own or that of our particular political group, so never mind what is going on in heaven. How often is it that daily bread is all we seek? As for forgiveness—it is in short supply.

As for deliverance from evil, the threat of nonexistence arising in the midst of a cancer pronouncement or the fear evoked by a catastrophic, life-threatening illness makes the cry for deliverance quite real. Deliverance is the subject matter in an acute care unit, even if unspoken. When you find yourself looking up at the ceiling from a hospital bed in the midst of monitors that shout out your blood pressure, heart rate, respiratory rate, and oxygen saturation on a continuous basis, being delivered from the fear of what might happen next looms large.

I have referred elsewhere to the psalms of lament as prayer that arises out of our greatest sense of abandonment. We might feel alone in the face of our deepest pain, so much alone that we cry out for divine presence. A feeling of being totally spent, down to our last emotional and spiritual nickel, might overtake us, and the "Our Fathers" start to roll from our lips. At such a time our theological understanding of Matthew 6:5–14 matters little as all we think and say is coming from deep within us, from a "gut level," perhaps the starting place of all earnest prayer.

And When You Pray

For most reading these words, an immediate threat of death is not the primary concern. Perhaps, rather, it is the evening news, with its images of political posturing, war, and gun violence on our streets. For what, then, should we pray? What might reflect God's kingdom in the now? Walter Brueggemann suggests we pray for justice as understood in the Bible. In doing so we must pray for and actively seek for all people everything that is needed for dignity, peace, freedom, health, joy, and security. He further argues that we should care enough to "nag" God.[1] We ask not once, but again and again. Then there is no room left for our selfish requests.

I recall praying in high school that God would give us victory in an athletic contest; I still hear such prayers today. But does God really care who wins a football game? I don't know, but I find I must join with Brueggemann, who offers the following examples of what we should petition God for in our daily prayers: "Dignity for children, safety for families, home for the homeless, health care for the poor, food for the needy, respect for the abused…women and children, compassion for men wearied too long, access for the disabled."[2] If the reader thinks such prayers are simply not needed or that the prayer is simply poetic and has no basis in reality, then consider the following: During my career in pediatric neurology, attending to victims of child abuse was an everyday occurrence. The children who ended up under my care had sustained significant head injuries either from being violently shaken or from direct trauma to the head. A diagnosis of "non-accidental head trauma" was most often used. Such a label reflected the intentionality of the injury without placing a more general label of "child abuse." These children presented with fractured skulls as well as other broken bones. Old fractures and evidence of twisting or torsion injury to the legs often appeared on the x-ray. CT scans of the brain most often revealed blood over the surface of and in the brain. The neurological outcomes of such injuries are devastating and often manifest as significant developmental delay or cerebral palsy along with mental retardation and epilepsy. At one point late in my career, I could have held an all-day clinic seeing only victims of "non-accidental head trauma."

Pray and Let Pray

Not infrequently, I am asked what it is that I do when I visit a hospitalized person. First, I knock on the door, and then I stick my head into the room to identify myself as a chaplain. It may be that the time is not good or a nurse or a therapist is present. And whether we like it or not, some folks just don't want a chaplain or a preacher in their room. Prior difficult experiences with organized religion or the church often drive such feelings.

The same enquirer wants to know if I pray or read Scripture. Yes, I do some of both—sometimes. But what I say in a prayer or how I say or lead the prayer varies as needed. There are times when saying a prayer aloud is, in a sense, contraindicated. There are folks who have not grown up around prayer so they are uncomfortable with it. Others simply don't want to share their prayer thoughts aloud. I always ask if the one in the bed would like to have a prayer. I use "have a prayer" in the sense of owning or possessing the prayer. I hope any prayer I might say aloud becomes the other's prayer as well. I usually ask what the patient would like to say in a prayer. More often than not, the one in the bed asks that we pray for her spouse and children, not her own comfort and cure.

If visitors are present, I like to invite them to join in the prayer. Some want to hold hands around the bed, a practice more often seen in the ICU, where life is often hanging in the balance. It is at this point that some of my most dramatic experiences in prayer have occurred. Not long ago, I stood at the bedside of a man dying from lung cancer. The end of his life was imminent. When I asked the family to join hands around the bed and started to pray, much to my surprise, everyone in the room except the patient started praying aloud; they were from a Pentecostal tradition. I have had that experience on several occasions, and I have loved it every time. It is hard to describe how I feel after such an experience. One of my Pentecostal friends says it is clearly the Holy Spirit. I have no reason to argue with that assessment.

It has been my experience on several occasions that the one I went to pray with turns the tables and prays for me, even in the face of her own suffering. About one year ago, I visited a middle-aged woman who had just learned ovarian cancer would soon take her life. She spontaneously announced her faith in God and asked if she could pray for me—yes, for me. Before I could conjure up an answer as I stood there with my mouth hanging open, she took my arm and started to pray for an anointing of the Holy Spirit and for my healing. She prayed for ten to fifteen minutes. When she finished, I was exhausted. I recall just sitting there stunned and looking at her through my now-moist eyes. How did she know? Or did she? Three days before this pastoral visit, I had received my MM diagnosis.

"I Just Pray—That's It"

The "emergency department" is aptly named. Its purpose is to render care as soon as possible when there is illness or injury that may be life-threatening. I arrived in the ED as resuscitation efforts on a suspected heart attack victim were under way. The man could not be resuscitated. His large family gathered in the hall and the family room. They had no warnings that this event was coming. He had been quite active and exercised regularly. Cries of "Why? Why?" filled the corridor.

One of the family members asked if I could contact their church, Southeast Christian Church, to see if one of the pastors was available. Such was not a problem, as my smartphone is chock-full of church phone numbers and the cell numbers of pastors, priests, and one imam. Fifteen minutes after my call, Ray Fryrear, one of the pastoral care staff, arrived. After a brief greeting I withdrew, leaving him with his church family. I returned about fifteen minutes later to find a changed mood, the room full of fairly calm folks hugging and comforting each other, and the pastor was gone.

A few days later, I ran into Ray Fryrear in the hospital corridor. I thanked him for coming so quickly, and I asked what he had done or said that day as the mood in the room had been transformed by his visit. He said, "I prayed. That is all I know to do." That was it, nothing else. He just prayed. Ray is in his eighties but looks younger. He always comes within a short period of time when called. I have jokingly told him that I thoroughly expect he will be found one day in his nineties lying belly up in the hospital parking lot with his hospital visitation list tightly in the grasp of both hands. He is living proof that God is still at the bedside.

Is God Still at the Bedside?

I see God in the woman clinging to her mother's hand as she tearfully speaks of approaching death and the loss she already feels.

I see God in family and friends gathered around the bed as life support is withdrawn and labored breaths announce the approach of life's final moments.

I see God in the Eucharistic minister who goes room to room each day to share the bread and wine.

I see God in the pastor who comes with holy trembling, so unnerved by the ICU trappings, but managing to greet, hug, and offer comfort and prayer.

I see God in the nurse who, though exhausted after a twelve-hour shift, stays with her patient who has no one else as he takes his last few breaths before passing into eternity.
I see God in the man now wasted away with end-stage disease and in horrific pain who extends a hand of greeting and asks how I am doing.

I see God at the bedside in the 81-year-old church staff member who comes to the ER on a moment's notice to simply embrace and pray with those gathered in grief.

I see God in the housekeeping lady who, upon encountering a woman sitting on the floor crying, tracks down a chaplain and, with authority, bids him go where he is needed.

I see God in a room now filled with anxious faces and blank stares waiting their turns to hear the word they do not want to hear.

I see God in the woman who says, "It has been eight years. I know my end is near. I am at peace." And her face reflects her words.

Why is it that I claim to see God in such places? Because that is where God has been known to hang out since the beginning.

Bill Holmes
July 2016

Notes

[1]Walter Brueggemann, *The Collected Sermons of Walter Brueggemann* (Louisville: Westminster John Knox, 2011), 98.

[2]Ibid.

CHAPTER 11

It's a Miracle! Or Is It?

"One man's coincidence is another man's miracle."
—Overheard in the ICU

I delayed my discussion of miracles as long as I could. No doubt in what follows I will cause objections to arise in the minds of more than a few readers. On the other hand it is my hope that before you are finished reading this essay, I will have put at least some of the objections to rest.

For the sake of a starting place, I will share a definition of "miracle" as found in the *Westminster Dictionary of Theological Terms*: "An event that is considered unusual or extraordinary in that it appears to be contrary to what is currently known of nature. Theologically, the emphasis is on what God has revealed through this event, as in the miracles of Jesus."[1]

Talk of miracles it is not uncommon in the halls and rooms of most hospitals. In thirty-seven years of practicing pediatrics and neurology, I frequently encountered expectations of a miracle or the perception that perhaps a miracle had already occurred. Such miracle talk came from some who had not necessarily ever identified themselves as people of faith. It is as though there is a cultural component disconnected from any notion of faith or belief. For some their religious preference was "None." Most, however, claimed to be a member of some faith-based group. Although I did not take a poll, my overall impression was that miracles were more talked about by conservative evangelical groups; that is not to say that mainline or more moderate churches had no or little notion of miracles.

It is not unusual in a medical setting for the groundwork for a miracle claim to be laid by the news of a poor prognosis. When the outcome is significantly better than prognosticated by the physician, claims of the miraculous follow. The patient, family, and friends had some conviction that through prayer and strong faith, God had been prompted to perform a miracle to act outside the laws of nature. Upon hearing these claims I am often prompted to think of those who are also praying people of faith but no miracle came to them and they lost their loved ones. Was God being arbitrary in this matter of granting miracles and choosing to answer one man's prayers but not another's?

Along this same line, as pastors and chaplains we should be aware that there is a point of "therapeutic futility," that place where it is no longer prudent or helpful to continue giving medication such as chemotherapy or to keep a person on life support when multiple organ failure is occurring. In some such instances we are only prolonging suffering. When medical treatment becomes futile, it does not mean there is nothing else to be done. While the medical team or hospice offers pain control, the faith community comes with prayer, listening as needed and supporting both the patient and the family. Further difficulties arise when someone "knows of a case" that did get better after being told they would not. More than a few times I have seen the frustration and anxiety of a patient or the family increase as they are thrown into a quandary by such reports. It behooves the teller to consider documenting the accuracy of such reports.

In a major pediatric referral center such as Norton Children's Hospital in Louisville, praying for a miracle to save a child from almost certain death was the rule, not the exception. Several years ago a four-year-old girl from rural Kentucky was riding an ATV with her father. At that time Kentucky led the nation in ATV sales and death and/or injury to children on ATVs. When the vehicle hit a log, she was thrown off as the ATV plunged into a culvert. In an unconscious state she was transported by air ambulance to Children's. Computerized tomography of her brain revealed diffuse bleeding and swelling. Shortly after admission to the pediatric ICU, she began to have seizures that proved very hard to control. For the next four or five days she was totally unresponsive with her only movements being the seizures. When her care team met with the family, her parents asked, "Doctor, how long do you think my child will have to be on a respirator? Will she wake up from this coma? What will she be like?" Unless I was confident of a good outcome, I usually gave a guarded or poor prognosis. I found it neither helpful nor wise to make optimistic statements in the face of all evidence to the contrary. In this little girl's case things did turn out to be better than predicted. Not unexpectedly her family, longstanding and devout members of a rural Protestant church, saw this as a miracle.

About ten years ago a middle-aged woman had a major stroke. The entire left side of her brain was markedly affected. This area controls speech and use of the right side of the body. Her neurologist offered a poor prognosis, suggesting that if she lived at all, she would be unable to either walk or talk. Six months later she was doing some walking and some talking and showing signs of steady improvement. Some saw this as a miracle from God even though they had made no specific request of God for a better outcome than predicted by the physician. As a neurologist I was prompted to see things from a purely pathophysiologic standpoint. I concluded that perhaps the damaged area of the brain was not as large as originally thought and as the brain swelling subsided, there was more recovery than expected. So it was that my immediate response to claims of the miraculous was to point to what we know of the natural process of what happens in any stroke. I reasoned that it was the lack of such knowledge plus the original poor prognosis that led some to say, "It is a miracle!" However, I kept my thoughts on the matter to myself. It was not a time to discuss the validity of miracle claims; it was a time to be thankful and rejoice.

It is quite tempting to be dismissive of the claims of the miraculous in our sophisticated postmodern world. We are able to scientifically explain many phenomena that at one time were said to be "miraculous." I expect that number to grow—a statement of faith? Nonetheless, many a devout person of faith will still declare his own faith and belief prompted God to perform a miracle even if I or anyone else can explain in medically scientific terms what happened. However, in this age of booming scientific knowledge, should I, or anyone else for that matter, set about proving or disproving miracle claims? Even in Jesus's time there were those who sought to deny the miraculous primarily by impugning the agent of the miracle. Recall that Jesus was accused of being a magician or an agent of Beelzebub.

Arguments aimed at proving or disproving someone's claim to have experienced a miracle are, for the most part, meaningless since what is being talked about is more of a mystical or transcendental experience that does not lend itself to the rigors of scientific dissection. Such experiences often come after a long period of suffering, uncertainty, praying, keeping vigil, and handholding. The weight of the moment is experienced more by the heart than the head. Even for those who have not had a track record of believing in God and God's promises, the experience of "This is a miracle!" may be quite real. The medical facts are not the issue; they take a back seat in the aftermath when life survives a storm.

It is worth noting that the Bible does not offer a sharp demarcation between the natural and the supernatural. There is not even a well-defined view of a miracle as a suspension of natural law. The various words we translate as *miracle* do not imply control by another world, heavenly or otherwise. Miracles in the Bible were not presented so future readers would be challenged to explain them or make them the subject of scientific investigation, but they were meant to point to God's power and grace, pointing beyond the event to the emerging kingdom of God. Perhaps at a later time someone may review the "facts" and see how things came out as they did, but even then, the experience of a miracle remains.

From time to time, both during my years of neurology practice and my service as a chaplain, I have encountered those who, in a sense, bargained with God for a miracle. I recall a small child who was pulled from a pond on his grandparents' farm. He was lifeless when his family, to the best of their ability, started resuscitation efforts immediately. By the time he arrived in the ED, he was still in a lifeless state but had a pulse, irregular respiratory efforts, and reactive pupils. When his overwhelmed family arrived, we had a prolonged discussion of the worst and the best of possibilities. I will never forget the father's words as he said, sobbing, "I am not sure I even believe in God, but if my son dies, I absolutely will not believe." Such "bargaining" with God is not infrequent during times of extreme stress and crises, but what, if anything, does this say about the relationship between faith and miracles? Are miracles experienced out of faith, or do miracles create faith? I do not seek an absolute answer based on close study of Scripture. My observations over two score years suggest it is a bit of both. More importantly, most of us, whether clergy or family, do not spend time deliberating such questions. Why? I think it is because we are consumed by either our grief or our gratitude, by our weeping or our rejoicing, and by our questioning God or our praising God.

So much have I seen claims of the miraculous arising from better-than-expected outcomes that I once said, "Most miracles are not so much miracles as doctors overly prognosticating." At one point in my life, I resisted labeling any event as a miracle. It had been my experience that, almost always, the claims of the miraculous fell apart under close scrutiny. Meanwhile, I arrived in the doctors' parking lot early each morning with prayers on my heart for guidance in the work of the day and for anything extraordinary God had to offer.

But now I find myself reconsidering those former feelings that bordered on being cynical. As a chaplain I now sit in the waiting room with those anxious to know what will happen to their loved ones. Now, entrenched with families in the foxholes of life, I begin to see things as they see them, and I relent in my claims of "not a miracle." When families receive encouraging news, see any improvement beyond the expected, feel any grasp of the hand in response to a loving touch, capture any grimace or eyelid flutter as words are spoke softly to a brain-injured loved one, or experience just about anything that is beyond the predicted, they may well say, "It's a miracle!" It is then I must still the voice of the neurologist who wants to say, "It was just a reflex. He does not really understand you or know you are present." The physician-prognosticator part of me wants to give the physiological reason why things seem better. What the neurologist perceives as reflex or predictable neurophysiologic change, the loving and caring parent, spouse, and friend see as "miracle." And the chaplain in me now says with them, "Yes!"

Even when the medical outcome is as bad as it could possibly be, I still see something of the miraculous. When families endure the unimaginable but somehow find new life in the midst of incredible loss, I see "miracle."

Yes, there are periods of doubt in the midst of the crises of life, but even as doubt is born, faith is delivering its finest hour. And we name it "miracle."

Thanks be to God!

Note

[1]"Miracle," in *Westminster Dictionary of Theological Terms*, ed. Donald K. McKim (Louisville: Westminster John Knox Press, 1996), 175.

CHAPTER 12

In Memory of A. Christopher Hammond (1951–2014)

In April 2012 the late Dr. Chris Hammond invited me to write for the Wayne E. Oates Institute online journal. Chris had dedicated several years of his life to keeping the Oates Institute vital and viable; it had become the focus of his life.

A few weeks before his death from cancer, Chris's good friend Dr. David Sawyer and I took Chris to his last Louisville Bats baseball game. He ordered a bratwurst and a beer even though he knew full well that neither would likely agree with his then-fragile stomach. We had arranged to have a scoreboard welcome for him at the end of the fourth inning. With one out in the bottom of the fourth, Chris announced it was time to go. David made the slowest wheelchair exit in history from Louisville Slugger Field. By the time we reached the turn to the exit, Chris's name was up on the scoreboard. David turned the wheelchair as I pointed to Chris's name. He managed a weak smile before we headed for the parking lot and home. I don't know which team won the game, nor does it matter. What mattered was that his brat stayed put.

Chris did not know then, nor did I, that he was inviting an avalanche of thoughts and written words that has not yet stopped. His request came at a time when I was again trying to discern the answer to "What now?" I was not yet ordained to the ministry. I was a part-time chaplain at Norton Brownsboro Hospital, working several days per week and keeping myself available to fill in when the full-time chaplain had to be gone. I was also preaching as needed in Baptist and Presbyterian churches as well as one Nazarene church. I was, in a sense, a relief pitcher. I chose "reliever" as the metaphor for what I was doing in life after thirty-seven years in medicine and four years preparing for ministry as pastor and chaplain.

I began each article with these words: "I confess that I have never been in the bullpen of a baseball park, but I have nonetheless found it to be a fitting metaphor for where I am in life now. It is the point in life where I am no longer a starter, but I am called into the game when what is needed is what I have to offer. Sometimes it is not my strikeout pitch or my 'best curveball ever seen'—but just my presence—that is needed. While sitting in the bullpen waiting my turn, I have time to read (while eating a hotdog), observe folks in the bleachers, or just reflect."

The second article I wrote was on solitude and loneliness. What follows is an expanded and somewhat modified version in memory of my baseball-loving friend Chris Hammond.

Solitude or Loneliness?[1]

It was early in the game when I looked up from my perch on the bullpen bench and noticed a familiar face. I knew the man from the barbershop, that great place of neighborhood information gathering—or is it gossip? He was in his eighties and did not have the greatest hearing. He, too, was a "reliever," as he cut hair a few days per month. He was sitting in the bleachers, no one to either side of him, wearing a cap and sunglasses, but unlike anyone else in the bleachers that day, he was reading a book. A cheer went up as the team's top hitter was announced, but he never looked up from what must have been a good read. He was in his own world, captivated by whatever the author had to say. In the midst of the crowd, he seemed to be experiencing solitude.

I suspect there were those a few seats away that wondered, as I did, why he was at the ballpark at all. Did loneliness drive him there? Was it the desire just to be somewhere among humans for a while? There are times that just having other people around allows some folks to focus on the task at hand. It is like playing the radio while you study.

I sometimes go to a nearby coffee shop, get a cup, and read for an hour or so. The room is often filled with others doing the same. Why do they come there? Is it just the free wifi connection? Perhaps, but I suspect it is more than that; I suspect that for some loneliness brings them there. Even if that is not the case, they appear to be alone in a crowded room, just as the man reading a book in the bleachers is alone in the baseball crowd, absorbed in his book. On the other hand, isn't it also possible that the man in the bleachers and folks in the coffee shop seek some sort of solitude?

I see solitude not as a state of being alone, perhaps not even a place of total quiet, but a "place" where I can listen for the voice of God. Wherever we find solitude, we need to go there as often as our souls require it, to listen even to the silence, for that so often is where we "hear" God speak. It is there that ineffable experiences, those that have no words to describe them, take place.

From time to time I take a personal retreat to St. Meinrad Archabbey in Indiana. The monks are in the Order of Benedict. Silence is not a requirement, but speaking softly and respecting the other's space is the order of the day. The first night there I spent nearly three hours in total silence, praying, reflecting, waiting, expecting. No reading. No listening to music. I was asleep early, then up at 4:30 a.m. to get to 5:30 lauds and vigils. As I walked out of the guest house at 5:15, heading to the Archabbey Church, the church bells were ringing. It was a clear and cool morning. A sense of expectation overtook me. Then, there I was, sitting with Benedictine monks, praying the psalms. For forty-five minutes I tried to do the "St. Meinrad sound," a distinct-sounding chant of the psalms. It is difficult to describe the peace I felt. It was an experience of prayer, both alone and in community, the likes of which I have rarely had and are difficult to explain. It was one of those moments that might fall under the "when it happens, you will know it" experiences. Ineffable? Perhaps, but certainly a sense that something was changing inwardly.

I left the church and took a long walk in the early morning chill. I began to have a renewed sense of the presence of God. Thoughts came to me that I believe to be "Spirit-induced." Gratitude filled my awareness. I believe I have been blessed with one opportunity after another that has prepared me for ministry. I believe all of these were gifts from God. Despite all of this, doubts and uncertainty remained ever present. The words that kept coming to me that morning were, "Keep going, one step at a time. I know you want to know the what, the where, and the how, but such are mine to give to you in due time. Cease your searching for absolute answers. Trust me!" There came over me a strong sense of "let your noisy heart be quiet and patient, for I am the Holy One. I AM who I AM."

In solitude we listen so we can hear God speak. Without solitude, life could be lonely, for it is there that community and service begin. It is in the hours of solitude that my inner wounds are slowly healed, my doubts struggle with my faith, my faith admits its weaknesses, and I find renewed purpose for the day.

As I wrote what now appears on this page, it dawned on me that this is what my youth minister at WSBC was trying to teach me as a teen when she repeatedly stressed the need for "time alone with God." Even at summer camps and retreats, time alone was a daily occurrence. Finding a tree to lean back on, then reading Scripture, thinking, and praying were expected of all of us. I didn't get it then, but now, sixty years later, I cannot live without it.

I saw my friend a few days later at the barbershop. I asked how he felt after his day at the ballpark reading a book. Then came the reply, "Great! I am ready to cut hair now." I get it.

Note

[1]Bill Holmes, "The View from the Bullpen: Solitude or Loneliness?" (Spring 2012). Used with permission of The Oates Institute, www.oates.org.

Afterthoughts

The "Technical Imperative"[1]

As I wrote the final draft of this book, I was being constantly bombarded by report after report of conflict at home and abroad. As a people we have had a difficult time finding our way in the barrage of charges and countercharges in the halls of power. As a nation we are facing threats from without and within.

In my lifetime I have seen science and technology used to do great harm and evil when it is in the hands of the powerful: gas chambers at Auschwitz, atomic bombs at Hiroshima and Nagasaki, napalm in southeast Asia, and the more recent drone and chemical warfare. The invention and development of the AK-47 and the subsequent assault weapons that have made their way into the hands of mentally impaired people and terrorists deserve mention.

With each destructive act, we as a society search for and usually find justification for creating and using more weapons—or so we think. Hundreds die at the hands of those brandishing assault weapons, but much of our country clings to an interpretation of the Second Amendment that probably was never intended by its writers, nor could they have foreseen its consequences with the advent of today's weapons.

Several years ago Darrell J. Fasching, a professor of religious studies, pointed out how post-Holocaust Jewish theologians tend to make a connection between Auschwitz and Hiroshima. There is revealed a "secularized technological civilization," which seems to have lost all sense of the sacred in life. He cites Jacques Ellul's term the "technical imperative," which says, "If it can be done, it should be done."[2]

Those who have followed or executed this "technical imperative" throughout history were not necessarily demons and evil people. Most often they were ordinary folks, like you and me, who seem to be able to justify their actions or disown their culpability. Like those who now appear in history books, we are capable of the best and the worst, individually and as a nation. We must, as a society of mostly caring and loving people, be vigilant and insist on accountability for what we do with our technology. We must always be vigilant and ask ourselves again and again, "Should we do this?" The answer should never be, "Yes, because we can."

Psalm 74 (Revisited)

I think we have a lot in common with God's people as revealed to us in the pages of the Hebrew Bible. The life of Israel met with disasters that affected the community: war; natural phenomena, such as famine and drought; and, for sure, the Babylonian destruction of the Jerusalem temple. Certainly the destruction of the very center of their worship left a community in disorientation and crying out as one to God.

As I read Psalm 74 recently, I tried to imagine how it might look today. Needless to say, I have not tried to do a line-for-line but sought to capture what I see as the mood of the psalm as it might speak to us today. I make no claim to theological or exegetical correctness. I know some, if not many, will disagree. I write as one who cries out at a gut level, "How long, O Lord, how long?"

O God, have you had it with us?
If these times are of you, why such anger?

Are we not the "saved" ones?
Has not your grace been "shed" on us?

If that is the case, then come! Come now!
See the carnage from without and within.

Those who would destroy us
have blown up our gathering places

With bombs and assault rifles.
They have desecrated your creation.

They have killed your creatures.
They have cursed and slaughtered the "not us."

They have sought to do away with the "other."
Or was it really "we" who did such?

If there are any prophets, they are silent.
If there are justice-seekers in high places, they are mute.

Those chosen to speak for us in the public forum
listen only to those who profit from instruments of death.

From East and West, North and South, Left and Right,
they come giving nothing but a deaf ear to the people.

You have parted great waters, stilled storms,
nourished your people of old in the barren wilderness,

changed water to wine, closed the lion's jaw,
called forth Lazarus, and made the lame to walk.

Still we have chosen to ignore Easter
and place our faith in Remington,

elevate Smith and Wesson to high places,
and thereby place our ultimate trust in our own "Baal."

We hear the incessant clamor of our adversaries,
some even claiming to represent you.

Do not forget your promise of presence, O Lord!
Do not forget the poor, the needy, and the downtrodden.

Surely the darkness of the day will flee your light
And the hatred of the hour will yield to your love.

Come, Lord Jesus! Come! Forgive us...forgive us...
for we have become the instruments of our own demise.

Bill Holmes
August 3, 2017

Notes

[1] Bill Holmes, "Ethical Reflection Should Inform Technology's Use," Ethics Daily, accessed August 31, 2017, http://www.ethicsdaily.com/ethical-reflection-should-inform-technologys-use-cms-21304. Used with permission.

[2] Darrell J. Fasching, "From Genocide to Global Ethics," in *Explorations in Global Ethics: Comparative Religious Ethics and Interreligious Dialogue,* ed. Sumner Twiss and Bruce Grelle (Boulder: Westview Press, 1999), 104.

CPSIA information can be obtained
at www.ICGtesting.com
Printed in the USA
LVOW10s0836220418
574298LV00006BA/25/P